# Marlene Koch's Unbelievable Desserts with Splenda Sweetener

# Also by Marlene Koch

*50 Splenda Recipes: Favorites from Fantastic Food with Splenda and Unbelievable Desserts with Splenda*

*Fantastic Food with Splenda: 160 Great Recipes for Meals Low in Sugar, Carbohydrates, Fat, and Calories*

*Low-Carb Cocktails: All the Fun and Taste without the Carbs (with Chuck Koch)*

*Unbelievable Desserts with Splenda: Sweet Treats Low in Sugar, Fat, and Calories*

*Marlene Koch's 375 Sensational Splenda Recipes: Recipes Low in Sugar, Fat, and Calories*

# Marlene Koch's Unbelievable Desserts with Splenda Sweetener

### Sweet Treats Low in Sugar, Fat, and Calories

## MARLENE KOCH

*Illustrations by Christopher Dollbaum*

*Photographs by Steve Legato*

*Food Styling by Carole Haffey*

**M. EVANS**

Lanham · New York · Boulder · Toronto · Plymouth, UK

Published by M. Evans
An imprint of The Rowman & Littlefield Publishing Group, Inc.
4501 Forbes Boulevard, Suite 200, Lanham, Maryland 20706
www.rlpgtrade.com

Estover Road, Plymouth PL6 7PY, United Kingdom

Distributed by NATIONAL BOOK NETWORK

**Library of Congress Cataloging-in-Publication Data**

Koch, Marlene.
     Marlene Koch's unbelievable desserts with Splenda sweetener : sweet treats low in sugar, fat, and calories / Marlene Koch ; illustrations by Christopher Dollbaum ; photographs by Steve Legato ; food styling by Carole Haffey. — Updated ed.
        p. cm.
     Includes index.
     ISBN-13: 978-1-59077-140-2 (cloth : alk. paper)
     ISBN-10: 1-59077-140-0 (cloth : alk. paper)
     ISBN-13: 978-1-59077-144-0 (e-book)
     ISBN-10: 1-59077-144-3 (e-book)
     1. Desserts. 2. Sucralose. I. Title.
TX773.K575 2009
641.8'6—dc22                                                                    2008038041

♾️ ™  The paper used in this publication meets the minimum requirements of American National Standard for Information Sciences—Permanence of Paper for Printed Library Materials, ANSI/NISO Z39.48-1992.

Manufactured in the United States of America.

This book offers food and beverages that should be enjoyed as part of an overall healthy diet and is not intended as a dietary prescription. Persons with health concerns should seek the advice of a qualified professional, such as a physician or registered dietitian, for a personalized diet plan. Even though the FDA has determined sucralose to be safe for everyone, persons consuming Splenda do so at their own risk. Neither the author nor the publisher is liable for the product and neither is in any way affiliated with the manufacturer, McNeil Nutritionals, LLC.

Splenda is a registered trademark of McNeil Nutritionals, LLC, a Division of McNeil-PPC Inc.

Weight Watchers and Winning Points are registered trademarks of Weight Watchers International, Inc. WW point comparisons have been calculated based on published Weight Watchers International, Inc. information and do not imply sponsorship or endorsement of such comparison.

*To all those who strive to be healthy,*
*yet still want to indulge in the sweet things in life.*

# Contents

# Acknowledgments

As with every book, I would first like to thank my sons Stephen and James for their love and support. Always willing to lend a mouth for tasting, they are my toughest critics (even for desserts) and inspire me with their honesty and genuine feedback. More thanks go to my husband Chuck, who beyond the tasting worked overtime for me in the kitchen and anywhere else required. And most important, I need to thank my sweet-loving stepdaughter Colleen, who continues to motivate me to create great-tasting foods that can easily fit into any meal plan.

The first edition of this book would not have been possible without the assistance of the many people whom I thanked then and would like to acknowledge again, most notably my friend, colleague, and editor extraordinaire P. J. Dempsey, who worked tirelessly to get my first book published and lent a hand again with this second edition. Thanks are also due to my current editor, Rick Rinehart, for his encouragement and support.

For helping me to take my ideas from concept to creation, I am grateful for my kitchen and editorial helpers. First I must give credit to the ever-cheerful demeanor and superb pastry skills of Sophia Ortiz. Far beyond her kitchen contributions, Sophia infused her enthusiasm for life, and all things sweet, not only into our home, but into our entire neighborhood. Additional thanks are due to Molly Zapp, who was there to lend support whenever it was needed—while easing the daily grind with her shy smile and calm manner.

For the addition of the photographs, which finally allow my readers to see just how beautiful healthy can be, I thank Steve Legato, Carole Haffey, and Joel and Cindy Beach. Photographer Steve Legato's mindful and discerning eye and calm demeanor, combined with food stylist Carole Haffey's incredible talent and organization, made the photo shoot delectable. Thanks to the Beaches—the setting was perfect.

My appreciation also extends to my family and friends, my anchors whose unyielding support guides me in all endeavors. And last, but not least, I am indebted to the hundreds of thousands of readers who have embraced my efforts to deliver good health with great taste!

# Introduction

It is with great excitement that I am able to offer once again this "unbelievable book." The original *Unbelievable Desserts with Splenda: Sweet Treats Low in Sugar, Fat, and Calories* was the very first book to feature the then virtually unknown sugar substitute sucralose (sold under the Splenda brand). In my introduction I made a bold statement saying that "Splenda is an amazing substitute for sugar." Now, seven years later, not only do I still wholeheartedly agree with my original opinion, but I'm pleased to say that millions of other users of Splenda products also agree with me. Splenda brand no-calorie sweetener (or "Splenda" as I refer to it in this book) has become *the* leader in no-calorie sugar substitutes. What's more, I have been able to continue to create not only sweet, delicious, satisfying treats, but a great range of foods that taste just as delectable as their high-sugar counterparts with this extraordinarily versatile product.

As a registered dietitian and professional cooking instructor, my personal discovery of sucralose came about as I was trying to create healthy low-sugar desserts for those with diabetes, including my own stepdaughter. After trying every other way I knew possible to create truly delicious low-sugar baked goods—without success—I was fortunate enough to discover sucralose shortly after it was introduced. As Oprah would say, this was my "a-ha" moment. This discovery not only launched me into a new career as a cookbook author, but I'm proud to say that it also changed the lives of over half a million people who have bought my books and are now able to enjoy foods they love—healthfully and guilt-free!

With the utmost appreciation, I would like to thank the readers who have cared enough to write to me and share their stories (and great reviews) about how very much they enjoy the recipes, and even more how the recipes and nutrition information has helped them and their families enjoy good health. I'm glad I was able to make a difference in your life through my books and am thankful you care enough to let me know.

Now, dare I say, of all the books I have written, it is this collection of dessert recipes that is closest to my heart. I'm not sure if it is because it was my first book or because it is chock full of all the classic delectable sweet treats that we all love. I still enjoy making and eating these recipes, which include many of my own family's favorites starting with my signature Unbelievable Chocolate Cake. Far beyond cake, the collection includes wonderful hot and refreshing cold beverages, irresistible home-style muffins and coffeecakes, delectable cookies and tasty cakes, picture-perfect blue ribbon pies and rich-tasting puddings and mousses, sensationally sweet sauces and terrific toppings, and last, but not least, an entire chapter on everybody's favorite dessert: cheesecake.

When I was asked to revise this book I wondered how I could top what I had already done, but once I set my mind to it, I came up with twenty-four brand-new recipes that should also become new family favorites. These tempting treats include refreshing Pomegranate Iced Tea, wholesome Sour Cream Blueberry Biscuits, trendy Two-Bite Lemon Poppy Seed Scones, five brand-new cookies, an incredible Ultra-Quick Triple Berry Crisp, several cool 'n' creamy mouthwatering sensations like luscious Strawberry Buttermilk Panna Cotta and Creamy Frozen Fruit Bars, a versatile Super Simple Cherry Topping, and two fabulous cupcake recipes: Black and White Cheesecake and classic Red Velvet!

What's more, you will find that I've gone back and revised the original recipes so that they now contain even easier to use instructions, new variations, and new, updated ingredients. I have also updated my "Low-Sugar Baking Secrets" to provide you with an understanding of what it takes to make everything that comes out of the oven picture perfect. All the same great nutritional information is included, and I've added a comparison to Weight Watchers' points for all my sweet-loving Weight Watchers' friends. Perhaps most exciting is what I feel is the icing on the cake (so to speak), and that is the addition of gorgeous full-color photographs that will help you see just how beautiful healthy can be. Enjoy!

# What Is "Splenda"?

Splenda is the brand name for a variety of products made from sucralose, the revolutionary, nonnutritive (no-calorie), sweetening product derived from sugar. Sucralose is made through a multistep patented process where chlorine atoms are substituted for three of sugar's eight hydrogen-oxygen pairs, resulting in a substance that tastes just like the sugar it is made from, minus the calories. Because pure sucralose is six hundred times sweeter than sugar, maltodextrin, a low-density carbohydrate derived from corn, is added to provide bulk and to enable it to measure cup-for-cup like regular table sugar. The resulting product may be familiar to you as Splenda No Calorie Sweetener, Granulated. (Sucralose is also mixed with sugar to create Splenda Sugar Blend for Baking, but you do not need it for the recipes in this book.)

What's so amazing about Splenda Granulated is that although it tastes like sugar, the body does not recognize it as sugar, so it is not metabolized—meaning that it's calorie free. (The bulking agents do provide a minute number of carbohydrate calories—five per tablespoon.) This also means Splenda Granulated has no effect on blood sugar or the secretion of insulin (which has been confirmed in studies done with those with diabetes). Sucralose is considered safe for people of all ages[1] and the proof is in the results of more than one hundred scientific studies conducted over a twenty-year period. In fact, you'll find no warning labels on Splenda products. At the time of this writing, sucralose has received approval for use in more than thirty countries throughout the world.

It goes without saying that, because of my science and health background, I only use products that I know are safe. But as a chef I also need to know that these healthful ingredients combine to make great-tasting food, and I'm happy to report that:

» Splenda Granulated tastes great.

» Splenda Granulated has a long shelf life.

» Splenda Granulated dissolves easily in beverages.

» Splenda Granulated does not have a bitter aftertaste, even when used in large quantities.

» Splenda Granulated can be used to bake!

---

1. Although sucralose is considered safe for everyone, pregnant women and children have special dietary needs that should be considered before adding sucralose to the diet. Consult your personal physician or registered dietitian for advice.

## Why Not Just Use Sugar?

Americans have an incredible sweet tooth. In fact, the affinity for sugar starts the day we're born. Ask any nurse the trick for getting a baby to take a bottle, and you may find it's a touch of sugar water on the nipple. The truth is that a little added sugar in the diet is not a problem. Sugar is not evil. Sugar is actually a good source of energy, and sweet treats are certainly an enjoyable part of everyday living, but the problem is that a *little* bit of sugar is not enough for most of us. Consider that the latest United States Department of Agriculture (USDA) Dietary Guidelines for Americans recommend that we consume and prepare foods and beverages "with little added sugars or caloric sweeteners."

### The Problem with Sugar

First, sugar promotes tooth decay. Second, sugar is full of calories—empty calories to be exact. Third, as added sugars[1] increase in the diet, either fewer calories are left for nutritious foods or weight gain occurs from the extra calories. In many sweet foods, with the exception of soda and some candies, sugar is often paired with fat, and this is clearly not desirable if you are concerned about your weight. Additionally, a diet high in added sugars may also boost triglyceride levels and adversely affect your blood sugar levels. Again, not exactly desirable for maintaining good health.

### How Much Sugar Is Too Much?

So what's a moderate intake of sugar? (See "Sugar—The Name Game" on page 13 for a listing of added sugars.) Most health organizations recommend that the average person consuming 2,200 calories a day limit his or her added sugar intake to less than ten teaspoons a day (or at the maximum less than 10 percent of your total calories).

Let's put that into perspective: A can of regular soda pop has ten to twelve teaspoons of sugar, as do many presweetened coffee drinks. A 4-ounce muffin has eight to ten teaspoons, a piece of frosted carrot cake has twelve teaspoons, and a piece of "light" restaurant cheesecake can have

---

1. Sugars that occur naturally in foods are not considered "added" and are not usually a concern for healthy individuals.

as much as fourteen teaspoons of added sugar. Is it any surprise that we are consuming 170 pounds of sugar per year (per person) in the United States?

On a daily basis, we average twenty teaspoons of added sugar, twice the recommended amount. That adds up to a whopping 110,000 calories a year—the caloric equivalent of thirty extra pounds!

## How Splenda Sweeteners Can Help

Desserts and sweetened beverages are by far the greatest contributors of added sugars in our diets. By using noncaloric sweeteners, such as sucralose, to replace sugars when possible, we can still enjoy the sweet treats we love without the extra sugar and calories. Splenda No Calorie Sweetener has only ninety-six calories per cup instead of sugar's 775. Now we really can have our cake and eat it, too!

# Diabetes

## What Is Diabetes?

My stepdaughter has type 2 diabetes. Since her diagnosis, Colleen has made many lifestyle changes. She has lost weight, watches the choices and portion sizes of the food she eats, and tries to get some exercise, but she has not lost her love for all the delicious sweet things in life. For her and the other twenty-four million Americans who have diabetes, sugar is an issue. Diabetes is a serious disease that affects the body's ability to metabolize glucose. Glucose is a type of sugar that is produced when either sugars or starches in any form are eaten. Insulin, a hormone secreted by the pancreas, is necessary for the body to utilize glucose for energy. In persons with diabetes, the body does not produce insulin, does not produce enough insulin, and/or the insulin does not work efficiently enough (due to insulin resistance of the cells). Without the proper amount of insulin, glucose (or sugar in the blood) accumulates above normal levels. This can have negative consequences in both the short and long term. For the person with diabetes, a healthy diet and sensible meal planning are important tools in managing their blood sugar levels.

## Does Having Diabetes Mean You Can't Eat Sugar?

It was once believed that persons with diabetes needed to eliminate all sugar from the diet. We now know that the rate at which a particular food affects the blood sugar depends on a lot of factors, and not simply its sugar content.[2] Based on this knowledge, new guidelines for diabetes management have been set forth by both the American Diabetes and Dietetic Associations. The emphasis is on the *total amount* and *quality* of the carbohydrates (carbs) one eats. Sugar can now be used as part of an overall healthy diet—and that's great news if you have diabetes and you love sweets.

As usual, there's a catch. When you consider a healthy diet that provides you with all of the nutrients you need, without excessive total calories and especially carbs, there just isn't much room for a lot of added sugar, especially since most people with type 2 diabetes need to reduce calories, not add more to their diets.

## Great Sweet Treats for Persons with Diabetes

Which brings me back to my stepdaughter—every day is a balance of good choices and good taste. Desserts, treats, sweet beverages—Colleen wants to enjoy them like everybody else. That means goodies that really taste like her old time favorites, not just "diet treats." She also enjoys having a whole piece of dessert (sometimes even more). She is delighted that I can now prepare many of her favorite foods and drinks again. Birthdays are no problem—I can make chocolate cake. Holidays are no problem—we can make pumpkin pie. Picnics are no problem—she can have a couple of chocolate chip cookies. Since Splenda Granulated has almost no calories and doesn't affect blood sugar, using it in these healthy recipes gives you the flexibility to meet your nutrition goals and, more importantly, to enjoy it!

# Do You Really Need to Lower the Fat?

I recently saw a so-called nutrition expert on television say that cutting the sugar out of your diet was all it took to stay slim and healthy. If that were true, it would be easy for me to put together rich tasting, good-for-you treats. In fact, I've seen recipes based on this premise: cream cheese, whipping cream, eggs, and sugar substitutes were the ingredients for a cheesecake. The sugar and carbohydrate content was low, but the fat load was outrageous. I analyzed one recipe. It contained 40 grams of fat per serving, which made up 93 percent of the calories. You may as well sit down and eat half a stick of butter!

---

2. The measurement of a food's effect on insulin and blood sugar levels is called its *glycemic index*. This is sometimes used to aid food selection for controlling weight and blood sugar.

## Fat Facts

No matter what the hype, it is important to remember the following facts have been scientifically proven to be true:

» Calories do count.

» Fat is dense in calories.

» A diet high in saturated and trans fats is not good for you.

## Lower Fat—Better Health

Most likely, if you're looking to reduce the added sugar in your diet, you want to lose weight, control your blood sugar, or improve your health. In each of these cases, consuming a lot of fat is not going to help you. Here's why:

» Fat is full of calories. Need proof? One gram of fat equals nine calories, whereas carbohydrate and protein have only four calories per gram. Many studies have been done on what it takes to gain or lose weight, and here is the truth: If you consume more calories than you burn, you will gain weight, but if you burn more than you consume, you will lose weight. It's that simple. High-fat diets are often higher in calories because foods high in fat have a lot of calories. Period. When you trim the fat, you can trim the calories.

» Fat can contribute to an increase in insulin resistance. It's true that when it comes to controlling your blood sugar, a *little* fat can actually be helpful. It doesn't create much of an insulin response, and it can help to slow the rise in blood sugar when it is eaten with foods high in carbohydrates. For example, ice cream raises your blood sugar less than sherbet; however, a rich ice cream has almost twice the calories. Those extra calories are important, because if you have diabetes and are overweight (as are 80 percent of persons with type 2 diabetes), losing weight is often a priority. Research shows that both abdominal fat and saturated fats in the diet can increase insulin resistance. So again, less fat is better for you.

» Saturated fat and trans fats have been implicated in increasing the risk for certain cancers as well as heart disease. For people with diabetes, this is of particular concern because they are at high risk for heart disease. Does all this mean that fat, not sugar, is the evil one and we can't have any? Of course not.

## How Much Fat Is Too Much?

The American Heart Association recommendation is to consume no more than 30 percent of your total calories as fat, with less than 10 percent from saturated fat and 1 percent from trans fats. In many weight loss programs, physicians and registered dietitians suggest no more than 25 percent of your calories should come from fat. For that average person consuming 2,200 calories, this would allow for a total intake of 61 to 73 grams of fat per day. (Remember, that means all your meals and snacks.) Currently, the American diet is closer to 34 percent than the maximum 30 percent recommended. And that 4 percent difference adds up to a lot of added calories and pounds every year. How do some favorite treats measure up? Well, a large muffin has 24 grams of fat, a brownie has 27 grams, a sticky bun at Mrs. Fields has 34 grams, and a piece of restaurant cheesecake has 50 grams. These same packaged cakes and cookies also contribute more than 40 percent of the trans fats in most diets. It might not be so bad if these foods were offering you a lot of nutrients, but they aren't.

## Low-Fat Yet Luscious

I'm particularly proud of the fact that even though I've managed to re-create many favorites—like carrot cake and cheesecake, chocolate chip cookies and coconut cream pie, and even some amazing cream puffs—that are low in fat (as well as in sugar and calories), they are still delicious. You'll be pleasantly surprised when you taste these treats because although they are low in fat, you'd never know it by tasting them.

# How to Interpret the Nutritional Analysis

The nutritional information that follows each of the recipes in this book has been calculated using Esha Nutrition Food Processor software. The nutrient content has been provided to help you make choices appropriate to your own needs and goals. Here are four points, along with my personal philosophy about the calculation of the nutritional information:

## 1. Real Portions

I have a real problem with healthy recipes that look "healthy" because the portion size is ridiculous. No, I'm not talking restaurant size, "I could barely finish it" ridiculous, I'm talking ridiculous as in minuscule. Portion size is an issue and we've all gotten a little too used to today's out of control, bigger-is-better mentality, but I have also seen dessert portions the size of a postage stamp in some popular healthy cookbooks and magazines. Okay, I'm exaggerating, but realistically, I have seen portions of cake cut smaller than the size of a credit card. I have found very few people satisfied with portions *that* small. Therefore, I have tried to find the middle ground: A nine-inch pie serves eight, a nine-inch cheesecake serves twelve, and a square cake pan serves nine when cut three by three and serves eight when cut no smaller than three by five, yielding fifteen satisfying bar cookies. (I actually saw one "healthy" recipe that yielded thirty-six bar cookies out of this size pan!)

## 2. Fat by the Numbers

Although I have previously mentioned the percentage of calories that should come from fat in foods, fat-percentage calculations in Splenda products need to be viewed differently. Fat percentage is a mathematical calculation: To calculate the percentage of fat in a product, you divide the calories that come from fat by the total number of calories. For example, if a muffin has 15 grams of fat—which equals 135 calories from fat (15 grams × 9 calories per gram = 135)—and a total of four hundred calories, the fat percentage would be 34 percent (135 fat calories ÷ 400 total calories = .34, or 34 percent). Thus, the greater the total calories, with fat remaining the same, the lower the fat percentage will be. If you raise the calories to five hundred in the muffins (without more fat), you will see the fat percentage drops (135 ÷ 500 = .27, or 27 percent). In fact, food manufacturers have been known to increase the sugar or carbohydrate in a product—instead of lowering the fat—to bring the fat percentage to or below 30 percent in order to call a food low-fat! What happens when you use Splenda Granulated is that the total number of calories goes down. That's good, but because the reduction is all from carbohydrate, it can make the fat *percentage* look high. A good example would be the Lemon Chiffon Pie. There are 170 (luscious) calories per piece; sixty of them come from fat—that's 35 percent. If I were to use sugar, the calories would be 240, and the fat calories would still be sixty. Now my pie is 25 percent fat, but the carbohydrate grams would double and the grams of sugar would triple! The bottom line is that all the recipes have acceptable levels of fat for maintaining good health and great taste. Their caloric content is significantly reduced from their full-fat counterparts, and both total fat and saturated fat are low.

## 3. Exchanges and Carbohydrate Counting

I have used the most current guidelines available to calculate the diabetic exchanges. You will find the exchanges rounded off to the nearest half. This was decided after consulting with a Director of Nutrition

Services and Certified Diabetes Educator for the Central Ohio Diabetes Association. She and I both feel that counting should be made easy, not confounding. I think you will be really amazed at how few exchanges you have to use to get real pieces of real desserts. I have been a nutritionist for many years, and these counts genuinely impress me. Of course, the total carbohydrate grams along with fiber are available for those counting carbs. I also included the actual sugar grams for those who are especially trying to reduce their intake of simple sugars. If you are concerned with the glycemic index of a food, remember that fat, fiber, and protein, when mixed with carbohydrate, all lower the glycemic index. A piece of pie that is moderate in fat and sugar will have a lower glycemic index than a very low-fat dessert that is high in sugar.

## 4. Desserts Are a Lot More Than Numbers

This the final word—relax. Peek at the numbers, but more importantly, enjoy. This is not meant to be a "diet" book but a book offering you an array of delectable treats that make eating fun! In fact, there isn't an item in this book that cannot be part of your healthy diet. How sweet is that?

## Sugars—Sweeteners and So Much More

### Sugar—The Name Game

Before I can talk about what sugar does, you need to know what sugar is. When most people hear the term *sugar*, they think of refined white sugar or sucrose. Sucrose is a simple carbohydrate and is the most commonly used sweetener. Sucrose includes both refined white and less refined brown sugars. But when bakers, nutritionists, or the USDA speak of *sugars*, they are referring to the wide variety of sweeteners found naturally in foods as well as the sugars added during food processing. That is what you will find on the sugar line of a food label and in the analysis of the recipes in this book. For instance, in my Apple Pie in a Bag recipe (page 84), no sugar (sucrose) is added, but it still contains 13 grams of sugar because apples—like other fruits and milk products—contain natural sugars. However, when we talk of curbing our intake of *added sugars*, we are speaking of all the simple sugars that we, not Mother Nature, add to foods. Added sugars include *brown sugar, confectionery sugar, corn syrup, fructose, fruit juice concentrates, glucose, honey, molasses, raw sugar, table sugar,* and *syrups.* This means that the "all-fruit" pie sweetened with concentrated fruit juice is actually quite high in added sugars! Marketers love to take advantage of the fact that only sucrose (whether refined like white sugar or less refined like brown sugar) is listed as sugar on many food packages.

### The Role of Sugars in Baking

The truth is that many types of simple carbohydrate or sugars are used to sweeten the treats we all love. In addition to sweetening, sugars or caloric sweeteners play many other roles in making recipes "work." Sugars:

» Aid in texture, structure, and/or volume.

» Add color by browning.

» Impart flavor.

» Give spread to cookies and thickness to sauces.

» Stabilize egg whites in meringues and egg foams.

» Enhance the appearance of the finished products.

» Provide a natural preservative quality by holding moisture.

» Give moistness and tenderness.

In baking, the type of sugar selected for a recipe is based not only on its ability to sweeten, but on the necessity for it to provide these additional functions for a particular desired outcome, that is, you pick the type of sweetener based on what you need it to *do* in the recipe. When it comes to low-sugar cooking and baking, *Splenda Granulated is excellent at sweetening.* It performs this particular function beautifully. Sucralose is made from sugar and therefore tastes like sugar. Splenda No Calorie Sweetener, Granulated, measures cup for cup like sugar and has no aftertaste (unlike saccharin), and it can take the heat (unlike aspartame). In beverages, cheesecakes, fruit pies, and many cold desserts, little modification (beyond lowering the fat content) was necessary to achieve wonderful results. That is because the main role of sugar in these types of recipes is to sweeten.

However, since Splenda Granulated is not a traditional sugar but a nonnutritive sweetener, additional adjustments needed to be made when working with many recipes. Although each recipe is unique, after working with Splenda sweeteners, I found there are some routine modifications that are helpful in order to get great results in low-sugar, low-fat baking, which I have outlined on pages 19–21 in "Low-Sugar Baking Secrets."

## Real Desserts Incredibly Low in Sugar

My goal is to create great-tasting, eye-appealing, healthful desserts that you will enjoy eating and be proud to serve. Many times, it is not possible to do so without *any* sugar of *any* type. I have been highly selective in using additional sugars in small quantities in recipes as needed. When they are used primarily for eye appeal, I have noted them as optional on the recipes. Because I have used them judiciously and have confirmed that the additional carbohydrate is minimal, I have already *included* these garnishes in the analysis of the recipes. Until I found Splenda sweeteners, I did not think it was possible to eliminate the quantity of sugar normally contained in these recipes with such great results. I think you will agree, like my tasters and the thousands who have been delighted with the first edition of this book, that to have delicious treats like these with a mere fraction of the usual added sugars is truly unbelievable.

# The Real Facts about Fats

## Know Your Fats

There are different types of fats just as there are different types of sugars. Unlike the various sugars, which affect the body similarly, fats are far from considered alike. Mono- and polyunsaturated fats are considered to be more healthful in the diet than saturated fat or trans fatty acids, which are often labeled as the "bad fats." In order to maintain your health, it is recommended that you limit the total amount of fat you eat. Equally important is to consume the types of fats that are more healthful. You can compare for yourself the differences between commonly used fats by referring to the chart below.

## Fat Facts

You may notice that all fats contribute similar calories. In fact, oils actually have more calories per tablespoon than shortening or butter. You may also note that butter, one of the most loved ingredients in baking, contains the highest amount of saturated fat while margarine contributes a small amount of trans fats. For this reason the total fat in all recipes has been reduced.

## Fat Facts *(per 1 tablespoon serving)*

| Fat Source | Calories | Total Fat | Saturated Fat | Trans Fat | Monounsaturated Fat | Cholesterol |
|---|---|---|---|---|---|---|
| Corn Oil | 120 | 14 | 2 | 0 | 4 | 0 |
| Canola Oil | 120 | 14 | 1 | 0 | 8 | 0 |
| Butter | 102 | 11.5 | 7.5 | 0 | 3 | 31 |
| Margarine | 100 | 11 | 2 | 2.5 | 5.5 | 0 |
| Marg 70% | 90 | 10 | 2 | 2.0 | 4 | 0 |
| Smart Balance Stick | 100 | 11 | 5.0 | 0 | 3.5 | 15 |
| Smart Balance Spread 67% | 80 | 9.0 | 2.5 | 0 | 3.5 | 0 |

## The Role of Fats in Baking

Despite its unhealthful qualities, butter is often a baker's number one choice because it has the best flavor of all baking fats. But fats also have many functions beyond their flavor. Fats:

» Give moistness and tenderness.

» Add flakiness to pastries.

» Carry other flavors.

» Are important for beating air into batters.

» Add smoothness.

» Contribute to "mouthfeel," providing that "melt in your mouth" sensation.

Solid fats, like butter and shortening, add different qualities to a recipe than liquid fats, like oil. For instance, while healthy oils are good for moistening, they cannot aerate, melt, or provide flakiness like solid fat. When reducing the total amount of fat, it is especially important that the fat you choose can do what you need it to do. This means sometimes using a healthy margarine when you need a solid fat and sometimes using a touch of butter when it makes a real taste difference. It also means choosing oil when moistness is the key and choosing shortening for a pie crust that is flaky, not tough. Whereas the fat can all but be eliminated in some recipes, in others, like cookies and pie crusts, some fat is clearly necessary to give a good-quality product.

There are lots of ways to reduce or switch the type of fat used when baking. You will find many ideas and techniques in the "Low-Fat Baking Tips" section on pages 18–19. You'll also notice substitutions made using dairy products. While not technically classified as fat, dairy products can contain a lot of fat. The technique not used, of course, is the addition of extra sugar to make up for the reduction in fat, a trick often used by food manufacturers.

## Fabulous Desserts with Less Fat (and Sugar)

Please read the "About the Recipes" section that follows before you begin making the recipes. It will give you many tips and a better understanding of the modifications necessary to make these wonderful treats. Go ahead, it's your turn to splurge!

# About the Recipes

## Measuring and Baking Basics

In order to help you get the best results from these recipes, I have included the following list of helpful hints. Because exact measurements and cooking temperatures are crucial to the success of baking more than in any other area of cooking, it is important that you follow the recipe instructions carefully. Read this section thoroughly before you begin.

### Measure Accurately

Use dry measuring cups for heavy, wet, or sticky ingredients like applesauce, yogurt, and molasses. Dry ingredients should be measured level with the top of the measuring cup or spoon by using a knife to sweep away the excess. It is important to loosen or aerate the flour first by stirring it with a spoon. Brown sugar should be packed firmly into the measuring spoon or cup.

Use a clear glass measuring cup for liquids. To get an accurate reading, make sure the cup is placed on the counter and read at eye level.

### Preheat Your Oven

Never begin baking in an oven that has not been brought up to the temperature specified in the recipe. Preheating only takes fifteen or twenty minutes. This important step should never be overlooked because it can literally make the difference between your recipe succeeding or failing. If you are unsure about the accuracy of your oven, invest in an oven thermometer.

### Cool Baked Goods Thoroughly

Use a rack for cooling to prevent excess condensation from forming on the bottom of baked goods.

### Store Baked Goods Properly

Wrap baked goods completely with plastic wrap or foil, or store in air-tight containers after they are thoroughly cooled. Although most reduced fat, reduced sugar homemade baked goods are at their best when they are the freshest, they will maintain their quality for two to three days when properly wrapped. Cheesecakes can maintain their quality very well for several days stored in the refrigerator.

To freeze, wrap cooled items tightly in plastic or foil before freezing. Thaw frozen items completely before unwrapping. Thawed baked goods can be heated in the microwave or oven to refresh them before serving. Muffins, quick breads, and plain cakes freeze well.

## Low-Fat Baking Tips

Lowering the fat in recipes without compromising taste is the goal of good low-fat baking. Eliminating *all* the fat is not the goal (although occasionally you can). I have lowered the fat in these recipes to healthy levels using the following tips. If you choose to make other substitutions in the recipes, your results will vary.

» The type of fat (butter, margarine, oil, etc.) used in a recipe is important to that recipe. Each has its own pluses and minuses in cooking as well as in your health. (See pages 15–16, "The Real Facts about Fat.") I use butter when the flavor greatly contributes to the recipe or when the amount is so small that the nutritional difference is negligible. Margarine can usually be substituted for butter to lower the saturated fat and cholesterol. Substituting oil for solid fats when they are specified is not recommended.

» Low-fat dairy products are richer and usually better tasting than nonfat, but some light products are still quite high in fat (like Neufchâtel cheese). In order to get the best outcome and still have the recipe be healthful, I often mix nonfat and low-fat ingredients together. You may choose to splurge further and use all low-fat products or even use some higher-fat ones. You can do so without affecting the quality of the recipe. I do not, however, recommend that the recipes be made with all nonfat products unless specified.

» Fruit and vegetable purées like applesauce, prune, pumpkin, and banana work well in adding moistness without fat. Although fruit purées do add carbohydrate, their natural sugars also help low-sugar baked goods rise. As a rule of thumb, fruit purées can easily replace one-half the usual fat in a recipe. Applesauce works best in lighter-tasting recipes, and prune purée gives great results in foods with stronger flavors—especially with chocolate. (I guarantee no one will ever know there are prunes hiding in any of these recipes!)

» Egg yolks add richness to recipes but also contain cholesterol and saturated fat. Therefore, I have minimized the use of egg yolks, using them only as necessary. The current guidelines for healthy egg consumption have been relaxed and allow up to one whole egg daily. Because I prefer the natural taste of whole eggs for baking, I use egg whites (no fat or cholesterol here) instead of egg substitutes. If you prefer, you may use a quarter-cup of egg substitute to replace two whites or one whole egg in recipes that do not require the egg white to be whipped.

» You may find the amount of spices and extracts in these recipes to be more than you would normally use. Fats give flavor and carry flavorings in foods, thus the additional spices and extracts in reduced-fat recipes ensure full-flavored treats and desserts.

# Low-Sugar Baking Secrets

*Please note that all the recipes in the book have been developed to work with the reduction of sugar and the use of Splenda Granulated sweetener.* The following secrets will help you to understand the science behind these recipes as well as how to make the adjustments required to invent your own true low-sugar, high-quality sweet treats. Since other nonnutritive sweeteners are not chemically identical to sucralose, they cannot be substituted for Splenda Granulated with the same results in every case. Nor can the Splenda packets except where specified (see the Splenda packet entry on page 25).

## Secret #1

*Sugar is sugar is sugar.* Honey, juice concentrates, fructose—all sugars. Don't be fooled by that "no-sugar cookie" full of honey. Your body knows what sugars are, and so should you. See page 13 for the reason manufacturers can make these claims and a listing of the different types of added sugars.

## Secret #2

A goal of *no* sugar in a dessert recipe is like there being no sand at the beach. That said, there are actually many great recipes in this book where no sugar of any kind has been added. However, there are also many recipes that use small amounts of different types of sugars. These sugars serve many functions beyond sweetening, and although the amounts are very small, they have been deemed necessary for a good-quality outcome. Additional reductions will be detrimental to the quality of the recipes. (See "The Role of Sugars in Baking," pages 13–14.)

## Secret #3

Sugar imparts volume to recipes. Since Splenda Granulated does not have the bulk of sugar, the volume and the weight of some recipes may be less. Adjustments need to be made to other ingredients (adding more), the pan size (using a smaller one), or in the case of drop cookies, the yield (making less), to make up for the loss of sugar. When creaming is called for, beating eggs and sugar and/or Splenda Granulated to its fullest volume will help to build extra volume and lightness in the recipe.

## Secret #4

When converting traditional recipes where sugar helps them rise (like cakes and muffins) to low-sugar versions, you may need to adjust the leavening. The manufacturer recommends one-half teaspoon of baking soda be added for each cup of Splenda Granulated. In recipes that already have a significant amount of baking soda, you can add less additional baking soda by adding more baking powder. Baking soda is high in sodium, which I find can negatively affect flavor in high quantities.

## Secret #5

Baked goods made with Splenda Granulated will cook faster. Check cakes up to ten minutes sooner, muffins five to eight minutes sooner, and cookies three to five minutes sooner.

## Secret #6

Drop cookies made with Splenda Granulated will not flatten as readily. Simply flatten them on the baking pan with the bottom of a glass or spatula before placing them in the oven.

## Secret #7

Since Splenda Granulated doesn't brown like sugar, the addition of small amounts of brown sugar, honey, or molasses will help in browning as well as contributing flavor. Some baked items may be lighter in color than their traditional counterparts. A light spritz of cooking spray on the top of baked goods before baking will also enhance browning.

## Secret #8

In recipes that have very little added sugar, the surface or crust can appear dull. To create a winning appearance, sprinkle the surface with a touch of granulated sugar before baking or powdered sugar after baking. Two teaspoons of sugar can coat an entire cake or batch of muffins, adding less than 1 gram of carbohydrate per serving.

### Secret #9

Use a small amounts of cornstarch to help thicken sauces that depend on sugar as the thickening agent.

### Secret #10

Some recipes are not as successful when converted to low-sugar versions. It is difficult to replace regular sugar when large amounts are required for volume and structure (such as angel food cake, pound cake, and simple meringue cookies), carmelization (such as candies and caramel sauces), or texture (pecan pie or cracked sugar toppings).

# Ingredients You Will Need

When creating low-sugar, low-fat treats, the exact combination of ingredients is crucial for great quality. Although you can make some substitutions in these recipes, you should use the ingredients specified in the recipe to ensure your treats taste as good as mine did and that the nutritional information I have supplied is accurate.

## Applesauce

Always use unsweetened applesauce. The sweetened varieties contain significant amounts of added sugar.

## Buttermilk

Regular buttermilk is low in fat. I use buttermilk labeled low-fat, but regular and nonfat varieties are also fine. The acidity of buttermilk helps to tenderize baked goods, and this is especially important when the fat and sugar in a recipe are low. You may also use powdered buttermilk, or you can substitute sour milk for buttermilk. To make sour milk, add 1 tablespoon of vinegar or lemon juice to a one-cup measuring cup. Add skim or 1% milk to fill the cup. Let stand for three minutes before using.

## Cake Flour

Cake flour has less protein than all-purpose flour. Fat and sugar both help to tenderize the protein in flour by inhibiting gluten formation. Because my cake recipes contain less fat and sugar, using cake flour produces a lighter, more tender cake. You'll find cake flour in the supermarket next to the flour; it's usually packaged in a box. The closest substitution would be to replace two tablespoons of each cup of all-purpose flour with cornstarch.

## Cocoa Powder

Dutch-processed cocoa powder is cocoa powder that has had some of the natural acidity of cocoa neutralized. It brings a darker, smoother cocoa flavor to recipes. Hershey's Special Dark and Droste can be found on the baking aisle, but any brand is fine. You may substitute regular unsweetened cocoa powder, but the color and cocoa taste may be less smooth in the finished product.

## Cream Cheese

Of all the ingredients I use I find cream cheese products to vary the most. I like Philadelphia cream cheese. The light cream cheese is sold in a tub. You can also substitute Neufchâtel cheese with good results, but it is higher in calories and fat. I also use Philadelphia nonfat cream cheese sold in an 8-ounce block. Mixing nonfat and low-fat cream cheeses together lowers the fat content while still providing good flavor. I find using nonfat cream cheese alone produces a very different product.

## Eggs

Although the risk of food-borne illness from eggs is very low, I recommend using pasteurized eggs or powdered egg whites in recipes where the egg white is not cooked long enough to ensure complete safety from the risk of salmonella poisoning for the elderly, people with compromised immune systems, or young children. Davidson's Pasteurized Eggs produces eggs pasteurized in their shell and JustWhites makes a great powdered egg white for meringues. Just follow the directions on the package for whole egg white equivalents.

## Flavorings

Real vanilla extract makes recipes taste better as do good-quality spices. Check your spices. If you can't smell them when you open the container, they are too old and should be replaced.

## Low-Sugar Jam

I have specified low-sugar jam because it contains no nonnutritive sweeteners, has half the sugar of regular jam, and has a wonderful fruit taste. The brand I have used is Smucker's. All-fruit spreads often contain concentrated fruit juices as sweeteners and are usually higher in sugar content (up to twice as much). Smucker's sugar-free jams may also be used.

## Margarine and Butter

With today's emphasis on reducing both saturated and trans fats, all of a sudden baking seems a bit tricky when it comes to health, but the fact is that solid fats *are a requirement in* many baking recipes. Even though you can't change the fact that solid fats are needed, you can substitute a healthier one. For example, one margarine I use for baking is I Can't Believe It's Not Butter, a 70 percent vegetable oil reduced-fat stick margarine. It contains 2.5 grams of trans fat but only 2 grams of saturated fat per serving for a combined total of 4.5 grams. Because the recipes use tablespoons, not cups of margarine, and that is spread out over many servings, every recipe is low in trans fat, saturated fat, and total fat. In contrast, commercially prepared foods often have several grams of trans fat along with additional saturated fat per serving. If you, however, prefer to eliminate all trans fat, Smart Balance brand makes trans fat–free butter blend sticks (with 5 grams of saturated fat) and a reduced-fat buttery spread (67 percent vegetable oil) that is not quite as solid, but is acceptable for baking. Watch that you do not choose any solid margarine or tub margarine with a fat content less than a 65 percent vegetable oil because these products will not work for baking as they contain too much water. Real butter may be used but will increase the total fat and, more specifically, the saturated fat content of the recipe. Last, only use light butter when specified. Light butter has the advantage of all the flavor with half of the fat of regular butter, but again, it has a high water content and is not suitable for all types of baking.

## Milk

I have specified 1% milk. At 20 percent fat, 1% milk fat is richer tasting than skim without the fat of 2% or whole milk. Skim milk can be substituted if you'd like, but the results will not be as creamy.

## Nonfat Half-and-Half

Nonfat or fat-free half-and-half has the creamy richness of half-and-half without the fat. Because it has more carbohydrate than regular half-and-half, I use it in small amounts. Many brands are now common. You can substitute regular half-and-half in the recipes; the grams of fat will be slightly higher. Do not substitute nonfat milk.

## Nonstick Cooking Sprays

There are two types of oil-based sprays I specify for coating pans. The first is a vegetable oil spray made from canola or corn that is unflavored, such as PAM. Be sure not to use an olive oil spray for baking because the flavor is too strong. The second type is nonstick *baking spray*, which contains a small amount of flour in the spray. This spray is great for cakes and other items that call for pans to be greased and floured. PAM makes one, as does Baker's Joy.

## Orange and Lemon Zest

Many recipes call for grated lemon or orange rind (zest). Simply grate the brightly colored outer layer off of the whole fruit. Use a box or sharp flat grater that has small holes to make a finely grated, but not mushy, zest. If the grated zest does not look finely minced, use a knife to finish it off before adding it to the recipe. Try not to use too much of the bitter white pith beneath the colored layer.

## Prune Purée

For prune purée I used to suggest a product called Sunsweet Lighter Bake; unfortunately, this is no longer available. Fortunately, you can easily make your own prune purée. Simply purée 1 cup of pitted prunes with 6 tablespoons of hot water in a food processor until smooth. Kept covered in the refrigerator it holds for 1–2 months. One tablespoon of purée replaces two tablespoons of fat in a recipe. Baby food prunes can also be used, but if they are not specifically called for in a recipe, the finished product will have a slightly cakier texture.

## Splenda Sweeteners

Splenda sugar substitutes can be found stocked next to the sugar. Splenda No Calorie Sweetener is available in packets and in the granulated form in boxes and baking bags. The granulated form measures cup for cup like sugar. The makers of Splenda products also now make a mix of granulated sugar and sucralose called Splenda Sugar Blend for Baking (where each cup has the sweetness of 2 cups of sugar). This product contains more calories and carbohydrates than the no-calorie sweetener due to its sugar content. Please note: *The recipes in this book were all formulated using Splenda Granulated, although Splenda packets may be substituted as indicated in many of the drink recipes. (Splenda packets have the sweetness equivalent to two teaspoons of sugar or of Splenda Granulated.)*

## Whipped Topping

Light whipped topping is found in tubs in the freezer section of supermarkets; be sure to thaw them before using. The nonfat versions of these toppings are not recommended because they are less creamy and have a higher sugar content.

## Yogurt

Plain low-fat yogurt may be substituted for the nonfat variety. Otherwise, use only the type of yogurt specified. If regular low-fat yogurt is specified, do not substitute "light" yogurt or artificially sweetened yogurts. The sweetness does not always hold up in baking. The recipes that do contain sweetened yogurt serve twelve, so the amount of sugar in each portion is minimal.

# The Recipes

# Hot and Cold Beverages

Ice Cold Lemonade

Cherry Berry Freeze

Pomegranate Iced Tea

Deep Dark Hot Chocolate

Vanilla Soy Chai Latte

Krista's Spiced Tea

Creamy Iced Coffee

Frosty Mocha

Strawberry Banana Smoothie

Berry Blast Smoothie

Orange Sunshine Smoothie

Oreo Cookies and Cream Milkshake

Ice-cold lemonade, steaming hot chocolate, fresh fruit smoothies, and cold and creamy milkshakes. There are times when the perfect thing to hit the spot is not something to eat at all—but something to drink. The choices today in beverages (and the calories they can pack) are astounding. Every week there's a new kind of beverage to choose from. Coffeehouses, smoothie bars, and lemonade stands always seem to be there just when you're ready for a little something. Unfortunately, a study from Purdue University has shown that when it comes to calories and extra pounds, those little somethings really add up. It seems that consuming fluid calories doesn't give us the same sense of fullness that comes from eating solid food, so we wind up consuming extra calories that quickly add up. And since most of the calories in these beverages come from sugar or fat, you're also not getting much nutritional bang for your buck. If you enjoy sweet drinks, here are some great waist-saving recipes for all your favorites. Best of all, these creations will definitely satisfy like their calorie-laden cousins because they taste just like them!

# Ice Cold Lemonade

*Serves One*

*Nothing beats the heat like cold lemonade. Unfortunately, the amount of sugar it takes to sweeten those lemons is enough to make you pucker. So, enjoy this sweet version without the added sugar or calories.*

INGREDIENTS:

⅓ **cup fresh lemon juice (1 large lemon) or ⅓ cup lemon juice concentrate**

**2 tablespoons Splenda Granulated sweetener (or 3 Splenda packets)**

**Crushed ice**

**Water**

STEPS:

1. Pour the lemon juice into a tall (12-ounce) glass. Add the sweetener and stir until dissolved.
2. Fill with crushed ice and cold water. Stir.

*Sweetened beverages are the number-one source of added sugars in the American diet. By simply switching over from regular lemonade, you save 25 grams of sugar and 100 calories for each glass.*

**PER SERVING**

Calories 30
Carbohydrate 9 grams
    Sugars 3 grams
    Fiber 0 grams

Total Fat 0 grams
    Saturated Fat 0 grams
Protein 0 grams
Sodium 0 milligrams

Diabetic exchange = ½ Fruit
WW point comparison = 1 point

# Cherry Berry Freeze

*Serves Two*

*My boys love this recipe! Bursting with the flavor of deep, dark cherries, this slushee-style drink is oh-so delicious and super easy to make. It's also a great choice if you prefer something nondairy and/or fat free.*

INGREDIENTS:

**1 cup light cranberry juice**

**1 cup frozen pitted dark cherries (without added sugar)**

**2 tablespoons Splenda Granulated sweetener (or 3 Splenda packets)**

**1–2 drops almond extract (optional)**

**½ cup crushed ice**

STEPS:

1. Place cranberry juice, cherries, sweetener, and optional almond extract into a blender.

2. Add ice and blend at high speed until ice is completely crushed and drink is slushy.

3. Pour into a tall glass and serve immediately.

*Cherries are high in vitamin C, potassium, antioxidants, and fiber. Perhaps more surprising is the fact that cherries have a low glycemic index and raise blood sugar more slowly than grapes, peaches, or blueberries.*

**PER SERVING**

| | |
|---|---|
| Calories 70 | Total Fat 0 grams |
| Carbohydrate 17 grams | Saturated Fat 0 grams |
| Sugars 8 grams | Protein 0 grams |
| Fiber 1.5 grams | Sodium 0 grams |

Diabetic exchange = 1 Fruit
WW point comparison = 1 point

# Pomegranate Iced Tea

*Serves Four*

*The popularity of pomegranate as an ingredient has exploded with the growing evidence of its health benefits. Although you can find the delicious and refreshing combination of pomegranate juice and tea available commercially in pomegranate teas, I have found that it's really easy to duplicate this drink at home for a substantial savings in money, calories, and, of course, unwanted sugar.*

INGREDIENTS:

3½ cups water

1 black tea or green tea bag

½ cup 100% pomegranate juice
  (like POM brand)

½ cup Splenda Granulated sweetener

STEPS:

1. In a tea kettle or pan, bring water to a boil. Add the tea bag and steep for 5 minutes. Remove the tea bag and discard.

2. Add pomegranate juice and sweetener.

3. Stir until well-mixed and let cool to room temperature.

4. Move to refrigerator and chill for 2–3 hours. Serve ice cold in a tall glass.

*Ounce for ounce, pomegranate juice has more natural antioxidants than any other juice, red wine, or green tea. You may use any brand you choose, but make sure it says 100% juice on the label.*

**PER SERVING**

| | |
|---|---|
| Calories 25 | Total Fat 0 grams |
| Carbohydrate 6 grams | Saturated Fat 0 grams |
| Sugars 2 grams | Protein 0 grams |
| Fiber 0 grams | Sodium 0 milligrams |

Diabetic exchange = ½ Fruit
WW point comparison = 1 point

# Deep Dark Hot Chocolate

*Serves One*

*I developed this recipe when my eldest son was eight. He called it "Mom's Special Recipe," and no other hot chocolate would do. There are many specialty sugar-free hot chocolate mixes, but I have yet to find one that wards off the chills with the rich, dark flavor of this original recipe. (This also makes a great cold chocolate milk—no heating required.)*

INGREDIENTS:

**1 tablespoon Dutch-process cocoa powder (like Hershey's Special Dark)**

**1 tablespoon + 2 teaspoons Splenda Granulated sweetener (or 3 Splenda packets)**

**2 tablespoons hot water**

**1 cup 1% milk**

STEPS:

1. Place the cocoa powder and sweetener into a microwaveable mug.

2. Add the hot water and stir until smooth.

3. Pour in the milk and stir again.

4. Microwave on high for 1½ minutes or until hot. (Do not boil.)

FLAVORED VARIATIONS: Try adding ¼ teaspoon of vanilla, orange, or raspberry extract.

*Did you know that an individual packet of hot chocolate can contain as much as 5 teaspoons of sugar?*

**PER SERVING**

| | |
|---|---|
| Calories 120 | Total Fat 3 grams |
| Carbohydrate 16 grams | Saturated Fat 2 grams |
| Sugars 11 grams | Protein 9 grams |
| Fiber 1 gram | Sodium 124 milligrams |

Diabetic exchange = 1 Low-Fat Milk
WW point comparison = 2 points

# Vanilla Soy Chai Latte

*Serves One*

*I find this Vanilla Soy Chai Latte to be the perfect midday "time out for Mom" drink to warm me up and get me back on track. It's also a great tummy warmer for a cold, dark, or rainy day (and no run to the local coffee shop is required).*

INGREDIENTS:

**1 chai tea bag**

**⅓ cup water**

**⅔ cup light unsweetened soy milk, plain or vanilla**

**1 tablespoon Splenda Granulated sweetener (or 1–2 Splenda packets)**

**1 teaspoon nonfat nondairy creamer**

**½ teaspoon vanilla extract**

STEPS:

1. Place the water in a microwaveable mug and microwave on high for 1 minute (or bring the water to a boil in a teapot and pour into a mug).

2. Steep the tea bag in the water for 3 minutes. Remove bag.

3. Stir in the remaining ingredients until well blended. Place mug back into the microwave for an additional minute (or warm in small pot) and serve.

*All soy milks are not alike! Be sure to look carefully for one that is unsweetened to reduce sugar (and calories). Some flavored soy milks contain as much as 22 grams of sugar per cup.*

PER SERVING

| | |
|---|---|
| Calories 80 | Total Fat 1.5 grams |
| Carbohydrate 12 grams | Saturated Fat 0 grams |
| Sugars 0 grams | Protein 3 grams |
| Fiber 0 grams | Sodium 65 milligrams |

Diabetic exchange = 1 Nonfat Milk
WW point comparison = 1 point

# Krista's Spiced Tea

*Serves Four*

*A friend and nutrition colleague of mine is a diabetes educator. She was kind enough to give me the recipe for a hot tea that she and her clients really enjoy. This tea reminds me of hot cider but has fewer calories and no added sugar. You'll find that Krista's Spiced Tea is great on its own, but even better when served with a nice warm biscuit or scone.*

INGREDIENTS:

**3 cups boiling water**

**3 cinnamon flavored tea bags**

**½ cup light orange juice**

**1 teaspoon lemon juice**

**⅓ cup Splenda Granulated sweetener**

STEPS:

1. Steep tea bags in water for 5 minutes. Remove tea bags and discard.

2. Add orange juice, lemon juice, and sweetener.

3. Stir and serve.

VARIATION: Serve cold with ice.

*This tea smells wonderful. For holiday entertaining, double or triple the recipe and place in a pot or crockpot to keep warm. Drop in a fresh cinnamon stick and a few twists of fresh orange peel as garnishes.*

---

**PER SERVING**

| | |
|---|---|
| Calories 15 | Total Fat 0 grams |
| Carbohydrate 4 grams | Saturated Fat 0 grams |
| Sugars 2 grams | Protein 0 grams |
| Fiber 0 grams | Sodium 0 milligrams |

Diabetic exchange = 1 Free Food
WW point comparison = 0 points

# Creamy Iced Coffee

*Serves One*

*It's amazing how popular coffee drinks have become. Many of my clients use them as an afternoon pick-me-up. The only problem is that these drinks are loaded with calories and sugar. In fact, a small coffeehouse drink often contains more sugar than a can of cola. Quick and easy to make, this version has a fraction of the calories (and cost!). The trick to getting a silky texture without sugar is to use nonfat half-and-half in place of milk.*

INGREDIENTS:

½ cup double-strength coffee or
  2 teaspoons instant coffee dissolved
  in 4 ounces of warm water (regular
  or decaffeinated)

¼ cup nonfat half-and-half

2 tablespoons Splenda Granulated
  sweetener (or 3 Splenda packets)

½ cup crushed ice

STEPS:

1. Pour the coffee, half-and-half, and sweetener into a blender. Blend to mix.
2. Add the ice and blend briefly (about 15 seconds) until ice is incorporated. Pour into an 8-ounce glass.

*A 9.5-ounce bottle of Starbucks Frappuccino contains 31 grams of sugar.*

**PER SERVING**

Calories 48

Carbohydrate 8 grams

  Sugars 4 grams

  Fiber 0 grams

Total Fat 0.5 gram

  Saturated Fat 0 grams

Protein 2 grams

Sodium 60 milligrams

Diabetic exchange = ½ Carbohydrate
WW point comparison = 1 point

# Frosty Mocha

*Serves One*

*This Frosty Mocha is a delicious twist on Creamy Iced Coffee. In addition to the chocolate, I've added more ice to make this 12-ounce version tall and frosty. Don't forget to have a straw ready.*

INGREDIENTS:

½ cup double-strength coffee or 2 teaspoons instant coffee dissolved in 4 ounces of warm water (regular or decaffeinated)

¼ cup + 1 tablespoon nonfat half-and-half

3 tablespoons Splenda Granulated sweetener (or 4 Splenda packets)

1 teaspoon unsweetened cocoa powder

1 cup crushed ice

STEPS:

1. Pour the coffee, half-and-half, sweetener, and cocoa powder into a blender. Blend to mix.
2. Add half of the ice and blend briefly (about 15 seconds) until ice is incorporated.
3. Add the rest of the ice and blend once more.
4. Pour into a tall 12-ounce glass.

*The good news about Au Bon Pain's Frozen Mocha Blast (16 ounces) is that it has only 3 grams of fat. The bad news is that, at 320 calories, it contains more than 60 grams of sugar.*

**PER SERVING**

| | |
|---|---|
| Calories 61 | Total Fat 0.5 gram |
| Carbohydrate 10 | Saturated Fat 0 grams |
|   Sugars 5 grams | Protein 2 grams |
|   Fiber 0 grams | Sodium 67 milligrams |

Diabetic exchange = ½ Carbohydrate
WW point comparison = 1 point

# Strawberry Banana Smoothie

*Serves Two*

*Whether you like your smoothies thick and creamy or cool and frosty, this recipe fits the bill. Perfect for a snack or as part of a meal, this soothing taste combination is always a winner. It also makes use of those overripe bananas—simply peel them and place them in a plastic bag before freezing. Frozen bananas will keep for a month or more.*

INGREDIENTS:

1 cup 1% (or skim) milk

1 cup plain nonfat yogurt

1 cup sliced strawberries (about 8 medium)

2 tablespoons Splenda Granulated
    sweetener (or 3 Splenda packets)

½ large banana (frozen)

STEPS:

THICK AND CREAMY:

1. Place milk into a blender. Add yogurt, strawberries, and sweetener. Pulse.

2. Add the banana and blend until thick and creamy.

COOL AND FROSTY:

1. Add 1 additional tablespoon of sweetener and ½ cup crushed ice to the thick and creamy smoothie.

2. Blend on high for 30 seconds longer until ice is incorporated.

*Add a scoop of protein powder to make a tasty high-protein shake or enjoy it with a handful of low-fat wheat crackers and a tablespoon of peanut butter for a wholesome low-calorie mini-meal.*

**PER SERVING**

Calories 150

Carbohydrate 24 grams

    Sugars 5 grams

    Fiber 2 grams

Total Fat 2 grams

    Saturated Fat 1 gram

Protein 10 grams

Sodium 65 milligrams

Diabetic exchange = 1 Low-Fat Milk, ½ Fruit

WW point comparison = 3 points

# Berry Blast Smoothie

*Serves Two*

*In a magazine, I saw a drink similar to this that was touted for its anti-cancer properties (berries have compounds that are powerful foes to tumors). But I love this drink mainly because of its delicious taste. Any combination of berries will do—just make sure one type is frozen.*

INGREDIENTS:

½ cup 1% (or skim) milk

1 cup plain nonfat yogurt

½ cup blueberries

½ cup frozen strawberries

¼ cup Splenda Granulated sweetener
  (or 6 Splenda packets)

1 cup crushed (or cubed) ice

STEPS:

1. Place milk in a blender. Add remaining ingredients except ice. Pulse.

2. Add ice and blend at high speed until smooth.

*By simply switching to lower-fat dairy products, I added 3 grams of protein and cut 5 grams of fat (4 saturated) and 20 calories per serving in this lean smoothie.*

---

**PER SERVING**

Calories 140

Carbohydrate 23 grams

  Sugars 18 grams

  Fiber 2 grams

Total Fat 1 gram

  Saturated Fat 0.5 gram

Protein 10 grams

Sodium 145 milligrams

Diabetic exchange = 1 Low-Fat Milk, ½ Fruit

WW point comparison = 2 points

# Orange Sunshine Smoothie

*Serves One*

*Reminiscent of a creamsicle, this creamy drink is a wonderful addition to any breakfast. It offers a full day's worth of vitamin C, with less sugar and more protein than even sunny orange juice can deliver.*

INGREDIENTS:

½ cup light orange juice

¼ cup plain nonfat yogurt

½ cup crushed (or cubed) ice

1 tablespoon Splenda Granulated sweetener (or 2 Splenda packets)

STEPS:

1. Place all ingredients in a blender.
2. Blend at high speed for 30–45 seconds.

*You may also use freshly squeezed or regular-style orange juice. This adds 30 calories, 6.5 grams of carbohydrate, and 1 additional Weight Watchers' point.*

**PER SERVING**

| | |
|---|---|
| Calories 70 | Total Fat 0 grams |
| Carbohydrate 13 grams | Saturated Fat 0 grams |
| Sugars 17 grams | Protein 5 grams |
| Fiber 0 grams | Sodium 145 milligrams |

Diabetic exchange = 1 Fruit, ½ Nonfat Milk

WW point comparison = 1 point

# Oreo Cookies and Cream Milkshake

*Serves One*

*Oreo cookies and ice cream, need I say more? This milkshake is perfect when you want to give the kids (or yourself) an extra-special treat. My son James considers this his new favorite milkshake (which is quite the compliment from a die-hard fast-food milkshake fan).*

INGREDIENTS:

½ cup lowfat 1% milk

½ cup light no-sugar-added vanilla ice cream

2 teaspoons Splenda Granulated sweetener (or 1 Splenda packet)

½ teaspoon vanilla extract

2 teaspoons dry nonfat creamer

¾ cup ice

½ pack (11 crisps) 100-calorie pack Oreos

STEPS:

1. Place milk, ice cream, sweetener, vanilla extract, and nonfat creamer in a blender. Blend just until all ingredients are combined.

2. Add ice and continue blending until thoroughly mixed and creamy.

3. Add Oreos and pulse a few times, just until the Oreos are incorporated throughout the milkshake.

4. Pour into tall, chilled glass and serve immediately.

*A 16-ounce Oreo shake at a fast-food restaurant averages 760 calories, with 40 grams of fat and 90 grams of carbohydrate, 70 of them from sugar! That's a whopping 18 points for my WW friends.*

PER SERVING

| | |
|---|---|
| Calories 160 | Total Fat 5 grams |
| Carbohydrate 24 grams | Saturated Fat 3 grams |
| Sugars 12 grams | Protein 6 grams |
| Fiber 2 grams | Sodium 180 milligrams |

Diabetic exchange = 1 Low-Fat Milk, ½ Carbohydrate
WW point comparison = 3 points

# Muffins, Coffeecakes, and Breakfast Breads

Let's face it—we all love to have a sweet treat to start the day. Muffins, coffeecakes, and sweet breads give us a legitimate excuse to do so. Unfortunately, most of them are simply filled with sugar and fat, which, of course translates into lots of calories. Because I also have a sweet tooth in the morning, I have taught classes and developed recipes to bring down the fat in these morning favorites. But when it came to reducing the sugar, things got tough. I remember making muffins for a group of children with diabetes and no matter how I tried, I had to use more sugar than I would have liked to get a good-quality, sweet-tasting muffin.

I am pleased to report that you can now have these treats—without the extra fat and tons of sugar—whenever you'd like. These were some of the first recipes I created, and I can't tell you how proud I was to have the owner of a bakery call in on national television to say these baked goods were truly "bake-shop" quality. Enjoy!

# Mega Muffin Mania

Somewhere along the line, something happened to the average-sized muffin—it's been replaced by supersized wonders just about everywhere! Not to say these monstrous muffins don't have appeal, obviously they do. It's just that instead of a snack or a quick breakfast bite, they've turned into full meals, and many people don't realize it.

Food-labeling laws state a serving of a muffin to be 2 ounces, but today's mega-muffins average 4 to 6 ounces. If you read the label carefully, you'll find your muffin may technically be considered 3 servings. This means if you multiply by 3 all the numbers on the nutritional analysis label, you now

have the real facts on these muffins that weigh in at 500 to 600 calories, with 18 to 24 grams of fat and as much as 90 grams of carbohydrate (that's six bread servings—ouch!).

The muffins here are made in traditional 2½-inch muffin tins (cupcake size). They are equivalent to a 2½- to 3-ounce muffin (baked goods with Splenda Granulated Sweetener weigh less than usual). If you want to splurge, you can bake them in the large, 3-inch wide tins and bake them 4 to 5 minutes longer. The recipes will make half as many, and you can simply double the nutrition information. With these healthy muffins, you can afford to.

## Muffin Comparison*

| Muffins | Calories | Fat Grams | Carbohydrate Grams | Sugar Grams |
|---|---|---|---|---|
| Regular Mega Muffin (6 oz.) | 540 | 24 | 72 | 42 |
| Low-Fat Mega Muffin | 480 | 9 | 94 | 54 |
| No Added Sugar Mega Muffin | 390 | 16 | 60 | 3 |
| Splenda Mega Muffin | 290 | 8 | 44 | 4 |
| Splenda 2½ oz. Muffin | 145 | 4 | 22 | 2 |

*Nutrient information from BJ's Warehouse Club and the average nutritional content of Splenda muffin recipes in this book

# Apple Oatmeal Streusel Muffins

*Serves Twelve*

*These are so good and good for you. I have made a few adjustments to the original recipe to lighten it up, but these tender muffins are still made with fresh apple and whole-wheat flour and topped with a streusel of oats and brown sugar. What a great way to start the day!*

## INGREDIENTS:

### STREUSEL TOPPING

2 tablespoons all-purpose flour

4 tablespoons rolled oats

2 tablespoons Splenda Granulated sweetener

1 tablespoon brown sugar

½ teaspoon cinnamon

1 tablespoon butter

### MUFFIN BATTER

1 large egg

1 cup low-fat buttermilk

3 tablespoons canola oil

¾ cup Splenda Granulated sweetener

1 cup peeled, grated cooking apple

1½ cups all-purpose flour

½ cup whole-wheat pastry flour

1 teaspoon baking powder

1 teaspoon baking soda

2 teaspoons cinnamon

¾ teaspoon nutmeg

## STEPS:

1. Preheat oven to 375°F. Spray standard 12-cup muffin tin with nonstick cooking spray.

2. STREUSEL TOPPING: Place all of the streusel ingredients except butter in a small bowl and stir until thoroughly mixed. Cut in butter until crumbly. Set aside.

3. BATTER: In a separate bowl, beat the egg with the buttermilk until foamy. Whisk in the oil, sweetener, and grated apple. Set aside.

4. In a large bowl, combine flour, baking powder, baking soda, cinnamon, and nutmeg. Make a well in the center and pour in the apple mixture. With a large spoon or spatula, stir just until dry ingredients are moistened.

5. Spoon batter into prepared muffin tin. Divide streusel evenly among muffin tops.

6. Bake for 15 minutes or until a toothpick comes out clean when placed into the center of the muffin. Remove from baking tin and cool on wire rack.

### PER SERVING

| | |
|---|---|
| Calories 150 | Total Fat 5 grams |
| Carbohydrate 22 grams | Saturated Fat 0.5 gram |
| Sugars 3 grams | Protein 4 grams |
| Fiber 1 gram | Sodium 180 milligrams |

Diabetic exchange = 1½ Carbohydrate, 1 Fat

WW point comparison = 3 points

# Best Bran Muffins

*Serves Eight*

*While everyone assumes bran muffins are good for you, most of them are chock-full of sugar and fat. Bursting with flavor, these dark and moist muffins pack a generous 5 grams of fiber, along with vitamin C and iron, without the stuff you don't want (or need). Like many muffins, they are at their best shortly after they are baked; however, you can make the batter ahead of time.*

INGREDIENTS:

**2 large egg whites**

**1 cup low-fat buttermilk**

**1½ cups 100% bran cereal (not flakes)**

**3 tablespoons molasses**

**2 tablespoons canola oil**

**1 teaspoon orange zest**

**½ cup all-purpose flour**

**½ cup whole-wheat flour**

**½ cup Splenda Granulated sweetener**

**1 teaspoon baking soda**

**1½ teaspoons baking powder**

**½ teaspoon cream of tartar**

**¼ cup finely chopped dried cranberries, raisins, or nuts★**

STEPS:

1. Preheat oven to 375°F. Spray 8 muffin cups in standard muffin tin with nonstick cooking spray.

2. In a medium bowl, whip the egg whites and buttermilk until frothy. Add the bran cereal, molasses, oil, orange zest, and cranberries, raisins, or nuts, if desired, and set aside for 5 minutes.

3. Measure flours, sweetener, baking soda, baking powder, and cream of tartar into a large bowl. Stir to mix. Make a well in the center and pour in the bran mixture. Using a large spoon or spatula, stir just until dry ingredients are moistened.

4. Spoon batter into muffin cups, filling ¾ full.

5. Bake for 18 minutes or until a center springs back when lightly touched. Cool for 5 minutes before removing to a wire rack. Store in an airtight container.

PER SERVING

| | |
|---|---|
| Calories 160 | Total Fat 4.5 grams |
| Carbohydrate 29 grams | Saturated Fat 0.5 gram |
| Sugars 10 grams | Protein 5 grams |
| Fiber 5 grams | Sodium 325 milligrams |

Diabetic exchange = 1½ Bread, ½ Fat

WW point comparison = 3 points

★ For dried fruit, add 3 grams carbohydrate and 12 calories per serving. For nuts, add 0.5 gram carbohydrate, 2 grams fat, and 24 calories per serving.

*Foods high in fiber help keep blood sugar levels on an even keel. The recommended guideline for fiber intake for adults is 28 grams per day on a 2,000-calorie diet.*

# Blueberry Muffins

*Serves Twelve*

*The most popular muffin? Why, blueberry, of course. These moist low-fat muffins are a breeze to make and a joy to eat. These can be made with frozen berries but are an extra-special treat when fresh blueberries are available. The lemon yogurt helps to keep them moist and adds a nice flavor.*

INGREDIENTS:

**1 large egg**

**3 tablespoons canola oil**

**½ cup Splenda Granulated sweetener**

**1 8-ounce cup low-fat lemon yogurt**

**6 tablespoons 1% milk**

**1½ teaspoons vanilla extract**

**2 cups all-purpose flour**

**1 tablespoon baking powder**

**½ teaspoon baking soda**

**1 cup blueberries (don't thaw if frozen)**

**1 teaspoon lemon zest**

**1½ teaspoons sugar (optional, for tops)**

STEPS:

1. Preheat oven to 375°F. Spray standard 12-cup muffin tin with nonstick cooking spray.

2. In a small bowl, whisk egg until frothy. Add oil, sweetener, yogurt, milk, and vanilla. Whisk until smooth.

3. In a large bowl, combine flour, baking powder, and baking soda. Stir. Add blueberries and lemon zest. Make a well in the dry ingredients and pour in the yogurt mixture. Using a large spoon or spatula, stir just until dry ingredients are moistened.

4. Spoon batter into muffin tins, filling each cup ⅔ full. If desired, sprinkle sugar lightly over muffins.

5. Bake for 18–20 minutes, or until center springs back when lightly touched. Cool for 5 minutes before removing to a wire rack.

*Do not substitute "light" or low-calorie lemon yogurt. The sugar in the regular low-fat yogurt helps the muffin sides and bottoms brown. Remember, each muffin has only a touch of sweetened yogurt in it.*

PER SERVING

Calories 145

Carbohydrate 23 grams

    Sugars 6 grams

    Fiber 0.5 gram

Total Fat 4.5 grams

    Saturated Fat 0.5 gram

Protein 4 grams

Sodium 200 milligrams

Diabetic exchange = 1½ Carbohydrate, ½ Fat

WW point comparison = 3 points

# Cranberry Orange Muffins

*Serves Twelve*

*The classic combination of orange and cranberries has become one of the most popular for muffins. The orange juice imparts a sweet and bold flavor and is a perfect complement to the tart cranberries. While these are great during the holidays when cranberries are in season, you can enjoy them year-round by keeping a few bags of cranberries in your freezer or substituting blueberries in the summer.*

## INGREDIENTS:

**2 cups all-purpose flour**

**2 teaspoons baking powder**

**½ teaspoon baking soda**

**¼ teaspoon salt**

**1¼ cups fresh cranberries**

**1 large egg**

**¼ cup canola oil**

**¾ cup light orange juice**

**½ cup 1% or skim milk**

**1 cup + 2 tablespoons Splenda Granulated sweetener**

**1 tablespoon orange zest**

**1 tablespoon reduced-sugar orange marmalade (optional)**

## STEPS:

1. Preheat oven to 375°F. Spray standard 12-cup muffin tin with nonstick cooking spray.

2. In a large bowl, combine flour, baking powder, baking soda, salt, and cranberries. Set aside.

3. In a small bowl, whisk the egg, oil, ½ cup orange juice, milk, 1 cup sweetener, and zest together. Make a well in the center of the dry ingredients and pour in the milk mixture. Using a large spoon or spatula, mix just until all the flour is moistened.

4. Spoon batter into the prepared tin and bake for 18–20 minutes or until center springs back when lightly touched.

5. While muffins are baking, place ¼ cup orange juice and 2 tablespoons of sweetener (and marmalade) into a small pot or microwaveable bowl. Heat gently until mixture reduces by half.

6. Remove muffins from the oven and brush each muffin with the orange mixture. Cool in the tin 5 minutes before removing to wire rack.

---

**PER SERVING**

| | |
|---|---|
| Calories 150 | Total Fat 5 grams |
| Carbohydrate 22 grams | Saturated Fat 0.5 gram |
| Sugars 3 grams | Protein 3 grams |
| Fiber 1 gram | Sodium 250 milligrams |

Diabetic exchange = 1½ Carbohydrate, 1 Fat
WW point comparison = 3 points

# Sour Cream Chocolate Chocolate Chip Muffins

*Serves Twelve*

*I must admit just seeing the word "chocolate" twice in the title is enough to make me take notice. This is "dessert for breakfast" at its best. These light, textured muffins are so rich with chocolate my son had me make them for his classroom for birthday treats. Serve them up with a nice glass of cold milk.*

## INGREDIENTS:

1½ cups all-purpose flour

⅓ cup Dutch-process cocoa powder (like Hershey's Special Dark)

1½ teaspoons baking powder

½ teaspoon baking soda

⅓ cup mini semisweet chocolate chips

3 tablespoons brown sugar

2 egg whites

3 tablespoons canola oil

½ cup unsweetened applesauce

⅔ cup 1% or skim milk

¼ cup light or nonfat sour cream

1 cup Splenda Granulated sweetener

1 teaspoon vanilla extract

2 teaspoons powdered sugar

## STEPS:

1. Preheat oven to 375°F. Spray standard 12-cup muffin tin with nonstick cooking spray.

2. Sift flour, cocoa powder, baking powder, and baking soda into a large bowl. Stir in chocolate chips. Add brown sugar. Set aside.

3. In a medium bowl, whisk egg whites until frothy. Stir in next 6 ingredients (oil through vanilla). Make a well in the center of the dry ingredients and pour in the liquid mixture. Using a large spoon or spatula, mix just until all the flour is moistened. Do not overmix.

4. Spoon batter into prepared muffin tin. Bake for 15–18 minutes or until center springs back when lightly touched. Cool for 5 minutes before moving to a wire rack.

5. Use a small sifter or mesh strainer to sprinkle powdered sugar over tops of muffins (this accounts for less than ½ gram carbohydrate per muffin).

*Two ways to incorporate the great flavor of chocolate into low-fat recipes is to use cocoa powder and mini chocolate chips (they disperse better so you can use less).*

## PER SERVING

| | |
|---|---|
| Calories 155 | Total Fat 6 grams |
| Carbohydrate 24 grams | Saturated Fat 1.5 grams |
| Sugars 7 grams | Protein 4 grams |
| Fiber 2 grams | Sodium 135 milligrams |

Diabetic exchange = 1½ Carbohydrate, 1 Fat

WW point comparison = 3 points

# Sour Cream Blueberry Biscuits

*Makes Twelve*

*Made with half whole-wheat flour and fresh blueberries, these light and tender, yet good-for-you biscuits are truly delicious. As with all biscuits, it is important once you add the milk to the flour mix that you do not overwork the dough or your biscuits will not be as tender. To make these quicker and eliminate re-rolling scraps of dough (as when making traditional round biscuits), you may pat the dough into a 12 × 4-inch rectangle, cut in half vertically, and then across five times to make twelve 2 × 2-inch square biscuits.*

INGREDIENTS:

1 cup all-purpose flour

1 cup white whole-wheat flour

1 tablespoon baking powder

¼ teaspoon baking soda

⅓ cup Splenda Granulated sweetener

1 teaspoon orange zest (rind of 1 orange)

3 tablespoons shortening

1 cup fresh blueberries, rinsed and drained

½ cup light sour cream

¾ cup 1% milk

1 large egg white, beaten

2 teaspoons granulated sugar

*For an even lighter biscuit, substitute 1 cup + 2 tablespoons cake flour for all-purpose flour.*

STEPS:

1. Preheat oven to 400°F. Coat a baking sheet with nonstick baking spray.

2. In a large mixing bowl combine the flours, baking powder, baking soda, sweetener, and orange zest.

3. Cut in the shortening with your hands, the tines of a fork, or a pastry knife. It is well blended when the mixture is a crumbly cornmeal-like consistency. Gently mix in blueberries. In a small bowl combine sour cream and milk. Add to flour mixture. With a spatula or wooden spoon, mix just until ingredients are moistened and form into a ball (dough will be a bit sticky).

4. Dust countertop with flour. Gently press down on dough and roll out to a ½-inch thickness. Using a 2½-inch round biscuit cutter, cut 12 biscuits. Place biscuits on a baking sheet. Brush tops with egg white and sprinkle lightly with sugar.

5. Bake for 13–15 minutes, until tops are shiny and golden brown. Transfer to a wire rack to cool slightly before serving.

**PER SERVING**

| | |
|---|---|
| Calories 140 | Total Fat 4.5 grams |
| Carbohydrate 21 grams | Saturated Fat 1.5 grams |
| Sugars 3 grams | Protein 4 grams |
| Fiber 2 grams | Sodium 240 milligrams |

Diabetic exchange = 1½ Carbohydrate
WW point comparison = 3 points

# Two-Bite Lemon Poppy Seed Scones

*Makes Twenty-Four*

*I love the fact that you can now find delicious bite-sized treats in the bakery section at many grocery stores, but I am amazed at how many calories can still be packed into something so small. My version of two-bite scones have less fat and fewer calories while the addition of a bit of whole-wheat flour makes them far more wholesome. With the tangy taste of lemon and a slight crunch from the poppy seeds, these scones may be small, but they are still big in flavor.*

INGREDIENTS:

**1 cup all-purpose flour**

**1 cup white whole-wheat flour (like King Arthur's)**

**½ cup Splenda Granulated sweetener**

**1 tablespoon poppy seeds**

**2 teaspoons baking powder**

**½ teaspoon baking soda**

**⅛ teaspoon salt**

**4 tablespoons margarine, very cold**

**6 tablespoons 1% milk**

**1 large egg**

**Zest of 1 lemon**

**1 teaspoon almond extract**

**½ teaspoon vanilla extract**

**2 teaspoons powdered sugar (optional)**

*Making perfect pasty is less of an art than you might think; using very cold margarine right out of the refrigerator makes all the difference!*

STEPS:

1. Preheat oven to 425°F. Coat a baking sheet with nonstick cooking spray.

2. In a large bowl, mix together the flours, sweetener, poppy seeds, baking powder, baking soda, and salt.

3. Cut in the margarine with your hands, the tines of a fork, or a pastry knife until the flour mixture resembles small crumbs.

4. In a small bowl, whisk together milk, egg, lemon zest, and extracts. Add to the flour mixture. With a spatula or wooden spoon, mix until ingredients are just moistened.

5. Dust countertop with flour. Gently roll out dough to a 12 × 4-inch rectangle. Cut rectangle in half lengthwise. Next, slice across strips at 2-inch intervals (you will have 6 pieces on each strip for 12 2 × 2-inch squares). Cut across each square diagonally to create 24 triangles. Place scones on baking sheet.

6. Bake for 13 minutes, until tops are lightly browned. Transfer to a wire rack to cool. Dust with powdered sugar before serving if desired.

**PER SERVING**

| | |
|---|---|
| Calories 60 | Total Fat 1 gram |
| Carbohydrate 9 grams | Saturated Fat 0 grams |
| Sugars 0 grams | Protein 2 grams |
| Fiber 0 grams | Sodium 160 milligrams |

Diabetic exchange = ½ Carbohydrate
WW point comparison = 1 points

# Quick Cake with Coconut and Almonds

*Serves Nine*

*This coffeecake is really quick! Light and tender, it takes advantage of a low-fat baking mix. The cake is mixed in one bowl and then topped with a yummy mixture of coconut and almonds before baking. Just add a Sunday morning paper and a cup of coffee and you're all set.*

INGREDIENTS:

1½ cups reduced-fat baking mix
  (like Reduced-Fat Bisquick)
½ cup + 2 tablespoons Splenda Granulated
  sweetener
½ teaspoon baking powder
⅔ cup 1% or skim milk
1 large egg, lightly beaten
1 tablespoon canola oil
½ teaspoon vanilla extract
6 tablespoons shredded coconut
1 tablespoon brown sugar
3 tablespoons sliced almonds
1 tablespoon melted margarine

STEPS:

1. Preheat oven to 350°F. Spray an 8-inch square baking pan with nonstick cooking spray.

2. Measure the baking mix, ½ cup sweetener, and baking powder into a large mixing bowl. Add the milk, egg, oil, and vanilla. Stir just until smooth. Spoon into prepared pan.

3. Place the coconut, 2 tablespoons sweetener, brown sugar, and almonds in a small bowl. Add the margarine and mix. Sprinkle this mixture over the top of the cake.

4. Bake for 20 minutes or until the center springs back when gently touched. Cool on rack.

*Switching to low-fat baking mix is an easy way to cut back on unnecessary fat.*

**PER SERVING**

| | |
|---|---|
| Calories 160 | Total Fat 7 grams |
| Carbohydrate 20 grams | Saturated Fat 2 grams |
| Sugars 5 grams | Protein 3 grams |
| Fiber 1 gram | Sodium 270 milligrams |

Diabetic exchange = 1½ Carbohydrate, 1 Fat
WW point comparison = 4 points

# Gingerbread Coffeecake

*Serves Eight*

*This tender and very light, textured cake may become your next Christmas classic. Not overly sweet, but with a subtle taste of gingerbread, it makes a fine treat after a hard day of holiday shopping.*

INGREDIENTS:

1 cup all-purpose flour, sifted

½ cup + 1 tablespoon Splenda Granulated sweetener

1¾ teaspoons cinnamon

¾ teaspoon ginger

¼ teaspoon allspice

4 tablespoons margarine

¾ teaspoon baking powder

½ teaspoon baking soda

½ cup buttermilk

1 tablespoon + 2 teaspoons molasses

1 large egg, lightly beaten

STEPS:

1. Preheat oven to 350°F. Spray an 8-inch round cake pan with nonstick cooking spray.

2. In a large bowl, combine flour with ½ cup sweetener, ¾ teaspoon cinnamon, ginger, and allspice. Cut in the margarine using a pastry blender or fork until the mixture resembles small crumbs. Measure out ⅓ cup into a small bowl and set aside.

3. To the large bowl of flour, add the baking powder, baking soda, buttermilk, molasses, and egg. Beat with a spoon or on low speed with a mixer until smooth. Spoon into the prepared pan.

4. Add last tablespoon of sweetener and 1 teaspoon cinnamon to the reserved crumb mixture. Sprinkle mixture over the top of the cake. Bake for 25 minutes or until the center of the cake springs back when touched lightly. Cool on rack.

PER SERVING

| | |
|---|---|
| Calories 130 | Total Fat 6 grams |
| Carbohydrate 17 grams | Saturated Fat 1.5 grams |
| Sugars 3 grams | Protein 3 grams |
| Fiber 0.5 gram | Sodium 200 milligrams |

Diabetic exchange = 1 Carbohydrate, 1 Fat

WW point comparison = 3 points

# Amazing Peaches and Cream Coffeecake

*Serves Nine*

*This amazing coffeecake takes only seven minutes to cook—in the microwave!
I, too, was a bit skeptical (okay, a lot skeptical) until I tried it. It's simply
amazing. Best served warm, this coffeecake is just right for a lovely brunch
on the patio. For a more traditional taste, make it using the vanilla extract;
but for me almond extract is the way to go.*

INGREDIENTS:

CAKE BATTER

**1½ cups all-purpose flour**

**½ cup Splenda Granulated sweetener**

**2 teaspoons baking powder**

**½ teaspoon baking soda**

**¼ cup brown sugar**

**⅓ cup butter**

**1 large egg**

**⅔ cup 1% milk**

TOPPING

**1 cup canned peaches in light syrup, rinsed
  and drained**

**⅓ cup light sour cream**

**⅓ cup nonfat half-and-half**

**2 tablespoons Splenda Granulated sweetener**

**½ teaspoon almond extract (or ¾ teaspoon
  vanilla extract)**

STEPS:

1. Lightly coat an 8-inch square microwavable dish with nonstick cooking spray.

2. In a large bowl, combine the flour, sweetener, baking powder, and baking soda. Set aside.

3. In a medium bowl, with an electric mixer, cream the sugar and butter together until light and fluffy. Add the egg and continue to beat until doubled in volume. Add the milk to the butter mixture and combine (the mixture will appear separated). Add the dry ingredients with a spatula or wooden spoon, mixing gently until smooth. Do not overmix. Pour batter into the prepared dish, using a spatula to level.

4. Arrange peaches on top of cake batter. Cover dish tightly with plastic wrap. Microwave on high for 4 minutes. Remove the plastic wrap and cook for another 3 minutes. Let it set for 5 minutes.

5. While cake is cooking, whisk together remaining topping ingredients in a small bowl. Pour sour cream mixture over warm cake and serve.

---

**PER SERVING**

| | |
|---|---|
| Calories 190 | Total Fat 8 grams |
| Carbohydrate 26 grams | Saturated Fat 4.5 grams |
| Sugars 9 grams | Protein 4 grams |
| Fiber 1 gram | Sodium 200 milligrams |

Diabetic exchange = 1½ Carbohydrate, 1 Fat
WW point comparison = 4 points

# Raspberry Almond Crumb Cake

*Serves Eight*

*This cake is picture perfect. Inspired by Cooking Light magazine, I retooled this delightful cream cheese and raspberry crumb cake, and lowered the sugar content to a mere 3 grams. Make it when you can get fresh raspberries and have a little extra time to put it together. This coffeecake is definitely worth it.*

INGREDIENTS:

**1 cup all-purpose flour, sifted**

**½ cup + 1 tablespoon + 1 teaspoon Splenda Granulated sweetener**

**4 tablespoons margarine**

**2 tablespoons sliced almonds**

**2 egg whites**

**1 teaspoon baking powder**

**¾ teaspoon baking soda**

**2 tablespoons 1% or skim milk**

**1 teaspoon vanilla extract**

**½ teaspoon almond extract**

**¼ cup low-fat cottage cheese**

**2 tablespoons tub-style light cream cheese**

**¼ cup low-sugar raspberry preserves**

**½ cup fresh raspberries**

*For egg whites to beat fluffy, be sure bowl and beaters are clean and grease-free and that no yolk gets into the whites. You don't need to wash the beaters before re-using them to beat the batter.*

---

**PER SERVING**

Calories 140

Carbohydrate 17 grams

  Sugars 3 grams

  Fiber 1 gram

Fat 6 grams (1.5 saturated)

  Saturated Fat 1.5 grams

Protein 4 grams

Sodium 230 milligrams

Diabetic exchange = 1 Carbohydrate, 1 Fat

WW point comparison= 3 points

STEPS:

1. Preheat oven to 350°F. Spray an 8-inch round springform or cake pan with nonstick cooking spray.

2. In a large bowl, combine flour and ½ cup sweetener. Cut in the margarine, using a pastry blender or fork, until the mixture resembles small crumbs. Measure out 6 tablespoons into a small bowl; add almonds and set aside.

3. Place the egg whites into a bowl and beat with an electric mixer until soft peaks form. Set aside.

4. To the large bowl of flour, add the baking powder and baking soda, milk, and extracts. Use mixer on low speed and beat until blended. Fold in the beaten egg whites with a spatula or large spoon and spoon batter into prepared pan.

5. Purée cottage cheese in a food processor until smooth. Add cream cheese and remaining sweetener and pulse again until thick and creamy. Spread evenly over the cake batter. Dot the cheese mixture with the preserves and top with the raspberries.

6. Sprinkle almond crumb mixture over entire cake. Bake for 20 minutes or until cake springs back when touched lightly in the center. Cool on rack.

# Blueberry Buckle

*Serves Nine*

*This is the perfect coffeecake for your next brunch. Bursting with blueberries, it's topped with a streusel flecked with orange rind and just a touch of sugar for a glistening appearance. Make it in the height of summer when blueberries are in season. Your guests will surely thank you.*

INGREDIENTS:

CAKE BATTER

1½ cups all-purpose flour, sifted

1½ teaspoons baking powder

½ teaspoon baking soda

½ cup Splenda Granulated sweetener

1 cup blueberries (½ pint)

2 tablespoons canola oil

1 large egg

¾ cup buttermilk

TOPPING

⅓ cup all-purpose flour

¼ cup Splenda Granulated sweetener

1 teaspoon orange zest

3 tablespoons light butter, chilled

2 teaspoons granulated sugar

STEPS:

1. Preheat oven to 350°F. Spray an 8-inch square baking pan with nonstick cooking spray.

2. BATTER: In a large bowl, combine 1½ cups flour, baking powder, and baking soda. Stir. Add ½ cup sweetener and blueberries.

3. In a small bowl, whisk the oil, egg, and buttermilk. Make a well in the center of the dry ingredients and pour in the buttermilk mixture. Stir briefly just to combine. Spoon into the prepared pan and smooth the top.

4. TOPPING: In another small bowl, place ⅓ cup flour, ¼ cup sweetener, and orange zest. Cut in the light butter until mixture resembles small crumbs. Sprinkle over the top of the cake. Sprinkle sugar over topping.

5. Bake for 20–23 minutes or until center springs back when lightly touched. Cool on rack.

*Just a touch of sugar, when spread on top, goes a long way and adds only 1 gram of carbohydrate per piece.*

**PER SERVING**

| | |
|---|---|
| Calories 160 | Total Fat 4.5 grams |
| Carbohydrate 26 grams | Saturated Fat 1 gram |
| Sugars 4 grams | Protein 4 grams |
| Fiber 2 grams | Sodium 190 milligrams |

Diabetic exchange = 1½ Carbohydrate, 1 Fat

WW point comparison = 3 points

# Cinnamon Streusel Coffeecake

*Serves Sixteen*

*This is the granddaddy of all coffeecakes. With streusel in the middle and on top, no wonder it's a favorite. The original has a stick or two of butter, sour cream, sugar, and nuts—so I knew I had my work cut out for me. But I finally came up with the big, showy cake I wanted. Wrap up this cake to seal in the moisture after you cut it. Less fat causes it to dry out faster.*

INGREDIENTS:

STREUSEL

⅔ **cup graham-cracker crumbs**

⅔ **cup Splenda Granulated sweetener**

⅓ **cup chopped nuts**

**2 tablespoons cinnamon**

**1 tablespoon canola oil**

**1 tablespoon brown sugar**

CAKE BATTER

**3 cups cake flour**

**1 tablespoon baking powder**

¾ **teaspoon baking soda**

⅓ **cup margarine**

1⅓ **cups Splenda Granulated sweetener**

**1 large egg**

**4 large egg whites**

**2 teaspoons vanilla extract**

½ **cup unsweetened applesauce**

1½ **cups light sour cream**

---

PER SERVING

| | |
|---|---|
| Calories 195 | Total Fat 8.5 grams |
| Carbohydrate 24 grams | Saturated Fat 3 grams |
|   Sugars 5 grams | Protein 5 grams |
|   Fiber 1 gram | Sodium 250 milligrams |

Diabetic exchange = 1½ Carbohydrate, 1½ Fat
WW point comparision = 4 points

STEPS:

1. Preheat oven to 350°F. Spray a 10-inch tube pan (angel food pan) or nonstick bundt pan with cooking spray.

2. STREUSEL: In a medium bowl, combine all the ingredients except the oil and brown sugar in a bowl. Set aside.

3. BATTER: Sift the cake flour, baking powder, and baking soda into a medium bowl. Set aside.

4. In a large mixing bowl, cream the margarine with an electric mixer. Add the sweetener and then the egg and continue to beat until smooth. Add the egg whites and vanilla. Beat briefly to incorporate. (It will not be smooth.) Beat in the applesauce. Add the sifted flour mixture and beat on low speed just until smooth. Add the sour cream and mix just until blended.

5. Spoon half of batter into the bottom of the prepared pan. Spread with a spoon to smooth. Sprinkle half of the streusel mixture over the batter. Drop the remaining batter by spoonfuls over the streusel and carefully spread. (Using the back of a spoon coated with cooking spray will help.)

6. Add the oil and brown sugar to the remaining streusel. Sprinkle on top.

7. Bake for 35–40 minutes or until a toothpick inserted near the center comes out clean. Cool on rack.

# Pumpkin Pecan Bread

*Serves Twelve*

*This holiday favorite is sure to please the most discerning of your guests. Serve it like I always do, with the crowd-pleasing Orange Cream Cheese on page 158 for a delicious taste treat.*

INGREDIENTS:

¼ cup canola oil

1 cup pumpkin purée

1 large egg

1 large egg white

½ cup low-fat buttermilk

2 tablespoons molasses

1 cup + 2 tablespoons Splenda Granulated sweetener

1¾ cups all-purpose flour

1 teaspoon baking powder

½ teaspoon baking soda

1½ teaspoons cinnamon

½ teaspoon ginger

¼ teaspoon cloves

⅓ cup chopped pecans

STEPS:

1. Preheat oven to 350°F. Coat a 9 × 5-inch loaf pan with nonstick cooking spray.

2. In a medium bowl, whisk together the oil, pumpkin, whole egg, egg white, buttermilk, molasses, and sweetener.

3. In a large bowl, measure the flour, baking powder, baking soda, spices, and nuts. Stir; make a well in the center and pour in the pumpkin mixture. With a large spoon or spatula, stir just until blended. Do not overmix.

4. Spoon the batter into the prepared pan and smooth surface.

5. Bake for 40–45 minutes until a toothpick or cake tester inserted into the center comes out clean. Cool on rack for 10–15 minutes and then remove from pan.

**PER SERVING**

| | |
|---|---|
| Calories 165 | Total Fat 7 grams |
| Carbohydrate 21 grams | Saturated Fat 0.5 gram |
|    Sugars 4 grams | Protein 4 grams |
|    Fiber 1 gram | Sodium 170 milligrams |

Diabetic exchange = 1½ Carbohydrate, 1 Fat

WW point comparison = 4 points (omit nuts and subtract 1 point)

*Did you know that one large bagel can have as much as 70 grams of carbohydrate?*

# Wholesome Banana Bread

*Serves Twelve*

*This banana bread is incredibly sweet, dense, and moist. It's also sturdy enough to pack and makes a great addition to anyone's lunch.*

INGREDIENTS:

1⅓ cups mashed ripe bananas (about 3 medium whole ripe bananas)

¼ cup low-fat buttermilk

1 cup all-purpose white flour

½ cup whole-wheat pastry flour

1 teaspoon baking soda

½ teaspoon baking powder

4 tablespoons margarine

2 tablespoons prune purée

1½ teaspoons vanilla

¾ cup Splenda Granulated sweetener

1 egg

*Fruit purées are great for adding moistness to quick breads without fat. Bananas have the additional benefit of being a great source of potassium.*

STEPS:

1. Preheat oven to 350°F. Spray one 9 × 5-inch loaf pan or two 6 × 3½-inch mini-loaves with nonstick cooking spray.

2. Mash the bananas in a small bowl by hand or with electric mixer. Stir in buttermilk. Set aside. In a medium bowl, sift together flours with baking soda and powder. Set aside.

3. In a large bowl, cream the margarine with an electric mixer on medium speed. Add the prune purée and beat well. Beat in the vanilla and the sweetener. Beat in the egg. On very low speed, alternate adding the banana mixture and the flour mixture, adding half of the flour and mixing until just incorporated and then half the banana. Repeat once.

4. Turn mixture into prepared pan(s) and smooth top.

5. Bake for 35–40 minutes for a 9 × 5-inch pan and 30 to 35 minutes for 2 mini-loaves or until a toothpick or cake tester inserted into the middle of the loaf comes out dry. Cool for 10–15 minutes on a rack and then remove from pan.

PER SERVING

| | |
|---|---|
| Calories 130 | Total Fat 4 grams |
| Carbohydrate 21 grams | Saturated Fat 1 gram |
| Sugars 6 grams | Protein 3 grams |
| Fiber 2 grams | Sodium 170 milligrams |

Diabetic exchange = 1 Carbohydrate, ½ Fruit, 1 Fat
WW point comparison = 3 points

# For the Love of Cookies

I've been baking cookies for as long as I can remember (I literally started as a child). Now I bake cookies with my kids. There are a lot of reasons I love baking cookies. Cookies are fun. Cookies are easy. Cookies can be tasted as soon as they are made! When I think of whipping up quick treats that are great to share, cookies are the answer. Yet, as I thought of creating winning baked goods that would be low in fat *and* sugar, cookies did not jump to the forefront. The truth is that most low-fat cookies are made with *extra* sugar to compensate for the reduction in fat. Sugar performs many functions in cookies in addition to making them sweet. Sugar also helps cookies to spread and makes them tender, brown, and crisp. In some cakey bar cookies, these attributes are not as important, but in standard drop cookies, these are the very qualities that make a cookie a cookie! Thus, you will find small amounts of sugar in all the drop cookies. Remember, when it comes to good health and good cooking, it's not about all or nothing, but balance. I have reduced the amount of added sugar in these low-fat cookies by 75 percent (or more), so instead of adding it by the cupful you add it by the spoonful. The result is a cookie that can compete with its full sugar and fat rivals. They look and taste wonderful (just ask my two cookie-gobbling kids) and can be enjoyed by everyone. Bake a batch and let the fun begin!

# Chocolate Chip Cookies
*Serves Eighteen*

*These chocolate chip cookies look and taste like the real McCoy. They are slightly soft, sweet, and full of chocolate. Jan from Phoenix recently emailed me that she bakes a batch of these just about every week. She is delighted that I've reduced the sugar by 75 percent and the fat by one-half, compared to the traditional recipe. But, most of all, she simply loves the cookies.*

INGREDIENTS:

**1 cup all-purpose flour**

**½ teaspoon baking soda**

**¼ cup margarine, softened**

**2 tablespoons prune purée★**

**⅔ cup Splenda Granulated sweetener**

**3 tablespoons brown sugar**

**1 large egg white**

**1½ teaspoons vanilla extract**

**6 tablespoons mini chocolate chips**

*If you substitute 1 tablespoon of corn syrup for 1 of the tablespoons of brown sugar, the outside of the cookie stays crisper, and you still average a mere 1 teaspoon sugar per cookie.*

★You may replace the prune purée with margarine. Your calories per cookie will increase by 5, and fat grams by 1. You reduce the carbohydrate content by 1 gram. See page 24 for the prune purée recipe.

STEPS:

1. Preheat oven to 375°F. Spray cookie sheet with nonstick cooking spray.

2. Combine flour and baking soda together in a small bowl. Set aside.

3. In a medium mixing bowl, with an electric mixer, beat margarine, prune purée, sweetener, and brown sugar until creamy. Add egg white and vanilla. Beat well. Stir in the flour mixture. Stir in chocolate chips.

4. Drop dough by level tablespoons onto cookie sheet. Press down on dough with the bottom of a glass or spatula to flatten.

5. Bake cookies for 4 minutes or until they "puff." Open oven and tap cookie sheet firmly against baking rack or the inside of the oven door to force cookies to drop and spread slightly.

6. Place cookies back in oven and bake 5 more minutes, or until lightly browned. Remove from pan and cool on rack. Cookies will remain crisp for several hours, then soften.

## Per Serving (1 Cookie)

| | |
|---|---|
| Calories 80 | Total Fat 3.5 grams |
| Carbohydrate 11 grams | Saturated Fat 1 gram |
| Sugars 5 grams | Protein 1 gram |
| Fiber 0.5 gram | Sodium 60 milligrams |

Diabetic exchange = 1 Carbohydrate, ½ Fat (2 cookies = 1½ Carbohydrate, 1 Fat)

WW point comparison = 2 points

# Better for You Chewy Chocolate Chip Cookies

*Makes Thirty*

*Entire books have been written about chocolate chip cookies. Here I simply offer a new alternative to my original Chocolate Chip cookies on page 63. These are for those who prefer a chewier, less cakey cookie. With all the great classic ingredients—real butter, sugar, chocolate chips, and even nuts—these chocolate chippers may be better for you, but they sure don't taste it!*

INGREDIENTS:

⅓ cup margarine or butter

¼ cup brown sugar

¼ cup sugar and ¼ cup Splenda Granulated sweetener (or ¼ cup Splenda Sugar Blend for Baking)

2 tablespoons prune purée

1 large egg

1½ teaspoons vanilla extract

1 cup all-purpose flour

½ cup white whole-wheat or regular whole-wheat pastry flour

¾ teaspoon baking soda

½ cup mini chocolate chips

¼ cup chopped pecans or walnuts

STEPS:

1. Preheat oven to 375°F. Spray cookie sheet with nonstick cooking spray.

2. In a large bowl, with an electric mixer, cream butter, brown sugar, sugar and sweetener (or Splenda Sugar Blend for Baking), and prune purée until very light. Beat in egg and vanilla.

3. In a small bowl, combine all-purpose flour, pastry flour, and baking soda. Mix to combine.

4. Add flour mixture to creamed mixture and beat to blend. Stir in chips and nuts.

5. Drop dough by level tablespoons onto baking sheet 2 inches apart. Flatten slightly with spatula.

6. Bake for 7–9 minutes or until set. Cool on baking sheet until firm. Remove to wire racks to finish cooling.

PER SERVING

| | |
|---|---|
| Calories 80 | Total Fat 4.5 grams |
| Carbohydrate 10 grams | Saturated Fat 1 gram |
| Sugars 4 grams | Protein 1 gram |
| Fiber 1 gram | Sodium 75 milligrams |

Diabetic exchange = 1 Carbohydrate
WW point comparison = 2 points

# Great Oatmeal Cookies

*Serves Twenty-Two*

*Here's another classic cookie-jar recipe. Many low-fat oatmeal cookie recipes replace some or all of the fat with applesauce, but I found that doing so, along with the significant reduction in sugar, gives you a very gummy cookie. My cookie uses butter for flavor, oil for tenderness, and prune purée for color and texture. The result is a low-fat, low-sugar cookie that is worthy of the cookie jar.*

## INGREDIENTS:

¾ cup all-purpose flour

1½ cups old-fashioned oats (not instant)

½ teaspoon baking soda

1 teaspoon cinnamon

2 tablespoons butter, softened

2 tablespoons canola oil

2 tablespoons prune purée

⅔ cup Splenda Granulated sweetener

3 tablespoons brown sugar

1 large egg

1 teaspoon vanilla extract

¼ cup dried cranberries, finely chopped

½ teaspoon orange zest

## STEPS:

1. Preheat oven to 350°F. Spray cookie sheet with nonstick cooking spray.

2. Combine flour, oats, baking soda, and cinnamon together in a bowl. Set aside.

3. In a medium mixing bowl, with an electric mixer, beat butter, oil, prune purée, sweetener, and brown sugar until creamy. Add egg and vanilla. Beat well. Stir in cranberries and zest and then flour mixture.

4. Drop dough, by level tablespoons, onto cookie sheet. Press down on dough with the bottom of a glass to flatten. Bake cookies for 4 minutes or until they "puff." Open oven and tap cookie sheet firmly against baking rack or the inside of the oven door to force cookies to drop and spread slightly. Place cookies back in oven and bake 5–7 more minutes, or until lightly browned.

5. Remove from pan and cool on rack. Cookies will remain crisp for several hours, then soften.

### PER SERVING (1 COOKIE)

| | |
|---|---|
| Calories 75 | Total Fat 3 grams |
| Carbohydrate 11 grams | Saturated Fat 1 gram |
| Sugars 3.5 grams | Protein 2 grams |
| Fiber 1 gram | Sodium 35 milligrams |

Diabetic exchange = 1 Carbohydrate, ½ Fat (2 cookies = 1½ Carbohydrate, 1 Fat)

WW point comparison = 2 points

*To make old-fashioned oatmeal raisin cookies, substitute raisins for the dried cranberries, eliminate the orange zest, and increase the vanilla and cinnamon by ½ teaspoon each.*

# Spiced Ginger Cookies

*Makes Twenty-Eight*

*These delightful chewy, spice-filled cookies are the perfect holiday gift cookie because they package so well. This is one cookie that I love to sample fresh from the oven, while they are still soft and warm. When cool, they crisp up a bit, but a fifteen-second pop in the microwave is all it takes to bring them back to soft and warm.*

INGREDIENTS:

¼ **cup shortening**

¼ **cup margarine**

1 **cup Splenda Granulated sweetener**

1 **large egg**

⅓ **cup molasses**

2 **cups all-purpose flour**

1 **teaspoon baking soda**

1 **teaspoon ground ginger**

1 **teaspoon ground cinnamon**

½ **teaspoon ground cloves**

STEPS:

1. Preheat oven to 350°F.

2. In a large bowl, with an electric mixer, cream the shortening, margarine, sweetener, egg, and molasses until light and creamy. Set aside.

3. In another bowl, whisk together flour, baking soda, and spices. Add to the shortening mixture. Mix well.

4. Roll dough by level tablespoon into balls and place 1 inch apart from each other on an ungreased baking sheet. Flatten cookies with the bottom of a glass cup, or press down on each ball with your middle three fingers to flatten and imprint a design.

5. Bake 10–12 minutes. Cool cookies on a wire rack.

**PER SERVING (1 COOKIE)**

Calories 80

Carbohydrate 11 grams

  Sugars 3 grams

  Fiber 0 grams

Total Fat 4 grams

  Saturated Fat 1.5 grams

Protein 1 gram

Sodium 0 milligrams

Diabetic exchange = 1 Carbohydrate

WW point comparison = 1 point

*Less refined than most sugars, blackstrap molasses is a very good source of several minerals, including potassium, calcium, copper, and iron.*

# Old-Fashioned Peanut Butter Cookies

*Serves Twenty-Six*

*Some of my most enjoyable cooking classes have been with children. My goal in selecting recipes is to choose foods kids love, in order to teach them the importance of good nutrition. These cookies provide a healthy alternative to junk food, and kids love 'em.*

INGREDIENTS:

1½ cups all-purpose flour

1 teaspoon baking soda

½ teaspoon baking powder

⅔ cup peanut butter

¼ cup margarine

2 tablespoons nonfat cream cheese

¾ cup Splenda Granulated sweetener

3 tablespoons brown sugar

1 large egg

3 tablespoons 1% milk

2 teaspoons vanilla extract

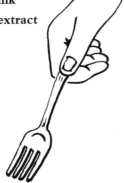

STEPS:

1. Preheat oven to 375°F. Spray cookie sheet with nonstick cooking spray.

2. Combine flour, baking soda, and baking powder together in a bowl. Set aside.

3. In a medium mixing bowl, with an electric mixer, beat peanut butter, margarine, cream cheese, sweetener, and brown sugar until creamy. Add egg, milk, and vanilla. Beat well. Stir in flour mixture.

4. Roll dough, by level tablespoons, into balls. Place onto cookie sheet and flatten with a fork forming a crisscross on top of each cookie.

5. Bake for 9–10 minutes. Remove from pan and cool on rack.

*Just add a glass of milk for a perfectly balanced after-school snack. Not only fun to eat— but also full of protein, "healthy" fat, and some carbs for energy.*

### PER SERVING (1 COOKIE)

| | |
|---|---|
| Calories 90 | Total Fat 5 grams |
| Carbohydrate 8 grams | Saturated Fat 1 gram |
|    Sugars 3 grams | Protein 3 grams |
|    Fiber 0.5 gram | Sodium 45 milligrams |

Diabetic exchange = ½ Carbohydrate, 1 Fat

WW point comparison = 2 points

# Chocolate Chocolate Chip Cookies

*Serves Twenty-Four*

*Chocolate and more chocolate—my kids think these are the best. Soft and oh-so-full of chocolate, these cookies benefit from the added milk, which helps them to spread nicely with only a touch of sugar.*

INGREDIENTS:

1 cup all-purpose flour

3 tablespoons Dutch-process cocoa powder (like Hershey's Special Dark)

½ teaspoon baking soda

⅓ cup margarine

2 tablespoons prune purée

½ cup Splenda Granulated sweetener

3 tablespoons brown sugar

1 egg

1 teaspoon vanilla extract

2 tablespoons 1% milk

⅓ cup mini chocolate chips

STEPS:

1. Preheat oven to 375°F. Spray cookie sheet with nonstick cooking spray.

2. Combine flour, cocoa, and baking soda together in a small bowl. Set aside.

3. In a medium mixing bowl, with an electric mixer, beat margarine, prune purée, sweetener, and brown sugar until creamy. Add egg and vanilla. Beat well. Stir in the flour mixture, alternating with milk. Stir in chocolate chips.

4. Drop dough, by level tablespoons, onto cookie sheet. Press down on dough with the bottom of a glass to flatten.

5. Bake cookies for 8–10 minutes. Remove from pan and cool on rack.

*Good news—chocolate is good for you! Studies show that the type of saturated fat in chocolate (stearic acid) does not raise cholesterol and that chocolate also contains healthful antioxidants. Therefore, moderate amounts of chocolate, especially dark chocolate, are now considered health food—who would've guessed?*

**PER SERVING (1 COOKIE)**

| | |
|---|---|
| Calories 60 | Total Fat 3 grams |
| Carbohydrate 8 grams | Saturated Fat 1 gram |
| Sugars 3 grams | Protein 1 gram |
| Fiber 1 gram | Sodium 30 milligrams |

Diabetic exchange = ½ Carbohydrate, ½ Fat

WW point comparison = 1 point

# S'more Cheesecake Bars

*Serves Fifteen*

*Remember making oh-so-yummy sticky s'mores when you were a kid? These decadent cheesecake bars add a bit of a twist making these s'mores a little more grown up, but still just as much a treat!*

INGREDIENTS:

CRUST

¾ cup graham cracker crumbs

¼ cup all-purpose flour

3 tablespoons Splenda Granulated sweetener

3 tablespoons margarine, cold

FILLING

8 ounces light tub-style cream cheese

½ cup nonfat cream cheese

⅔ cup Splenda Granulated sweetener

¾ teaspoon vanilla extract

1 large egg

1 large egg white

⅓ cup light sour cream

½ cup mini chocolate chips

*These luscious lightened-up bars have one-half the fat and carbohydrates and 40 percent fewer calories than the original recipe.*

STEPS:

1. Preheat oven to 325°F. Coat an 8-inch square pan with nonstick cooking spray.

2. In a large bowl, mix together flour, graham cracker crumbs, and sweetener. Cut in the margarine with your hands, the tines of a fork, or a pastry knife to form a fine crumb mix. Press mix evenly into bottom of prepared pan. Bake crust for 5 minutes and set aside.

3. In another large bowl, beat the cream cheeses with an electric mixer until smooth. Add the sweetener and vanilla extract and beat until well blended. Beat in the egg and egg white just until smooth. Stir in sour cream with a spoon.

4. Pour filling onto crust and spread evenly in pan. Sprinkle top evenly with chocolate chips and gently press into filling.

5. Bake mixture for 22–23 minutes or until center is set (it should still be slightly soft and will firm upon cooling). Cool at room temperature for 20 minutes and then place in the refrigerator for 2 hours to set. Once cheesecake is thoroughly chilled, cut into bars.

**PER SERVING**

| | |
|---|---|
| Calories 130 | Total Fat 7 grams |
| Carbohydrate 13 grams | Saturated Fat 4 grams |
| Sugars 8 grams | Protein 4 grams |
| Fiber 1 gram | Sodium 170 milligrams |

Diabetic exchange = 1 Carbohydrate, 1 Fat

WW point comparison = 3 points

# Creamy Lemon Cheesecake Bars

*Serves Twelve*

*I've seen some terrific low-fat lemon bar recipes. They may be low in fat, but the sugar—wow! There is sugar in the crust, more sugar in the filling, and, of course, they are topped with even more sugar. My lush lemon cheesecake bars are a wonderful alternative with less than half the calories, one-third the fat, and one-quarter the sugar content. Be sure not to overbake these or the creamy filling may crack.*

INGREDIENTS:

CRUST

**½ cup all-purpose flour**

**½ cup graham-cracker crumbs**

**2 tablespoons brown sugar**

**3 tablespoons Splenda Granulated sweetener**

**4 tablespoons cold margarine**

FILLING

**¾ cup low-fat cottage cheese**

**½ cup tub-style light cream cheese**

**¾ cup Splenda Granulated sweetener**

**1 tablespoons all-purpose flour**

**½ teaspoon baking powder**

**½ teaspoon vanilla extract**

**1 tablespoon lemon zest**

**3 tablespoons lemon juice**

**1 large egg**

**1 large egg white**

STEPS:

1. Preheat oven to 350°F. Spray an 8-inch square baking pan with nonstick cooking spray.

2. In a medium bowl, mix flour, graham cracker crumbs, brown sugar, and sweetener.

3. CRUST: Cut in margarine until mixture resembles fine crumbs. Press into prepared pan and bake for 15 minutes.

4. FILLING: Place cottage cheese in a food processor and purée until very smooth. Add the remaining ingredients, except egg and egg white and blend until smooth. Add egg and then egg white, pulsing just briefly to incorporate.

5. Pour filling over hot crust. Return to oven and bake for 18–20 minutes, or until cheese mixture appears just set.

---

**PER SERVING (1 BAR)**

| | |
|---|---|
| Calories 135 | Total Fat 6 grams |
| Carbohydrate 14 grams | Saturated Fat 2 grams |
| Sugars 5 grams | Protein 4 grams |
| Fiber 0 grams | Sodium 180 milligrams |

Diabetic exchange = 1 Carbohydrate, 1 Fat

WW point comparison = 3 points

*Traditional lemon bars use as much as 1½ cups of sugar for the same size recipe, which gives you 24 grams of sugar in every bar.*

# Apricot Oat Bars

*Serves Fifteen*

*These compact bar cookies are filled with the goodness of oats and the delectable taste of apricot jam. Because these cookies travel well, they would make a nice addition to your next picnic or potluck.*

INGREDIENTS:

½ **cup all-purpose flour**

½ **cup graham-cracker crumbs**

1 **cup old-fashioned oats (not instant)**

½ **cup Splenda Granulated sweetener**

⅓ **cup margarine**

¾ **cup low-sugar apricot preserves**

1 **tablespoon brown sugar**

*Try any of your favorite low-sugar jams or preserves in these bars but remember that "all fruit" or "no sugar added" does not necessarily mean low sugar. Check the nutrition label; Smucker's Low-Sugar Apricot Preserves contain only 6 grams of sugar per tablespoon as opposed to the usual 12–14.*

STEPS:

1. Preheat oven to 350°F. Spray an 8-inch square baking pan with nonstick cooking spray.

2. Place flour, graham-cracker crumbs, oats, sweetener, and margarine in a food processor. Pulse several times until the mixture resembles coarse crumbs.

3. Press ⅔, or about 2 cups, of the mixture into the prepared baking pan.

4. Bake for 15 minutes. Remove from oven and spread preserves over hot crust.

5. Add 1 tablespoon of brown sugar to remaining oat mixture, and spread oat layer over jam. Press down lightly on oats layer.

6. Bake for 20–25 minutes, or until lightly browned. Cool in pan on wire rack.

**PER SERVING (1 BAR)**

| | |
|---|---|
| Calories 115 | Total Fat 4 grams |
| Carbohydrate 17 grams | Saturated Fat 1 gram |
| Sugars 7 grams | Protein 2 grams |
| Fiber 1 gram | Sodium 60 milligrams |

Diabetic exchange = 1 Carbohydrate, 1 Fat

WW point comparison = 2 points

# Frosted Pumpkin Bars

*Serves Twenty-Four*

*Looking for a new holiday cookie recipe that is healthier than the rest? Here you go—these festive, cake-like pumpkin bars are sweet, moist, and very delicious. The finishing touch is the rich-tasting cream cheese frosting. All this and half your daily dose of vitamin A—it's enough to make you want to celebrate.*

## INGREDIENTS:

### COOKIE BARS

**2 cups all-purpose flour**

**1 teaspoon baking powder**

**½ teaspoon baking soda**

**1½ teaspoons cinnamon**

**½ teaspoon nutmeg**

**¼ teaspoon mace**

**6 tablespoons margarine, softened**

**1 2½-ounce jar baby food prunes**

**1 15-ounce can pumpkin purée**

**⅔ cup Splenda Granulated sweetener**

**2 tablespoons molasses**

**1½ teaspoons vanilla extract**

**1 egg**

**¼ cup raisins, finely chopped**

### FROSTING

**4 ounces tub-style light cream cheese**

**6 ounces nonfat cream cheese**

**¼ cup Splenda Granulated sweetener**

**2 tablespoons orange juice**

---

### PER SERVING (1 BAR)

| | |
|---|---|
| Calories 75 | Total Fat 3.5 grams |
| Carbohydrate 8 grams | Saturated Fat 1 gram |
| Sugars 3 grams | Protein 3 grams |
| Fiber 0.5 gram | Sodium 120 milligrams |

Diabetic exchange = ½ Carbohydrate, 1 Fat

WW point comparison = 2 points

## STEPS:

1. Preheat oven to 350°F. Spray a 9 × 13-inch pan with nonstick cooking spray.

2. Mix together flour, baking powder, baking soda, and spices.

3. In a large bowl, with an electric mixer, cream the margarine and prunes together. Add pumpkin purée, sweetener, molasses, vanilla, and egg. Beat well. Stir in flour mixture. Stir in raisins.

4. Spoon into prepared pan and smooth. Bake for 20 minutes, or until cake springs back when lightly touched in the center. Cool on rack.

5. In a small bowl, with an electric mixer, beat all frosting ingredients until smooth and fluffy. Spread frosting onto cool bars.

6. Refrigerate.

*In order to reduce the impact of an ingredient (whether the flavor or the nutritional consequence), you can eliminate it, substitute something else for it, or use less, like I did here. Because finely chopping the raisins disperses them better, you don't need as many, which helps to keep the sugar content low in this seasonal favorite.*

# Raspberry Shortbread Triangles

*Serves Nine*

*These pretty cookies remind me of an afternoon tea. They are quite attractive and rather tasty. Because the shortbread really stands out, I use butter in the crust for optimal flavor.*

INGREDIENTS:

CRUST

**1 cup all-purpose flour**

**6 tablespoons Splenda Granulated sweetener**

**½ teaspoon lemon zest**

**¼ cup butter**

**2 tablespoons light cream cheese or buttermilk**

TOPPING

**½ cup raspberry low-sugar preserves**

**½ cup fresh or frozen (partially thawed) raspberries**

**¼ cup Splenda Granulated sweetener**

**1 large egg white**

**1 teaspoon butter**

**⅛ teaspoon almond extract**

**⅓ cup sliced almonds**

STEPS:

1. Preheat oven to 350°F. Spray an 8-inch square pan with nonstick cooking spray.

2. CRUST: In a medium bowl, mix together flour, sweetener, and lemon zest. Cut in butter. Mix in cream cheese or drizzle in buttermilk until you have fine crumbs.

3. Press onto the bottom of the prepared pan. Bake for 15 minutes.

4. TOPPING: In a medium bowl, with an electric mixer, beat preserves and remaining ingredients except almonds. Pour over hot, baked crust. Return to oven for 15 minutes longer.

5. Open oven and sprinkle almonds evenly over top. Continue to bake 10 minutes longer.

6. Cool on rack 15 minutes. Divide into 9 squares by cutting 3 × 3; then cut each square in half to form 18 triangles.

---

**PER SERVING (2 COOKIES)**

| | |
|---|---|
| Calories 150 | Total Fat 7 grams |
| Carbohydrate 19 grams | Saturated Fat 4 grams |
| Sugars 7 grams | Protein 3 grams |
| Fiber 1 gram | Sodium 65 milligrams |

Diabetic exchange = 1 Carbohydrate, 1½ Fat

WW point comparison = 3 points

# Strawberry-Filled Thumbprint Cookies

*Serves Sixteen*

*Thumbprint cookies are a holiday tradition. The name "thumbprint" comes from the fact that your thumb can be used to create the indent, but personally I find my forefinger works much better. Either way, be sure to make the indent deep enough as it fills in partially while the cookies bake. Here I have chosen to use strawberry jam, but raspberry also works very nicely.*

INGREDIENTS:

1 cup all-purpose flour

½ teaspoon baking soda

½ teaspoon grated lemon peel

4 tablespoons margarine, softened

1½ tablespoons light corn syrup

½ cup Splenda Granulated sweetener

1 teaspoon vanilla extract

¼ teaspoon almond extract

1 large egg

3 tablespoons low-sugar strawberry preserves

STEPS:

1. In a small bowl combine the flour, baking soda, and lemon peel. Set aside.

2. In a medium bowl, with an electric mixer, beat margarine and corn syrup until creamy. Beat in sweetener and extracts. Add egg and beat again until well mixed. (Mixture will not look completely smooth.)

3. Add flour to mixture; mix well and form into a ball. Refrigerate for 30 minutes.

4. Preheat oven to 375°F. Roll dough into 1-inch balls and place on cookie sheet.

5. Press thumb or finger into the center of each ball to create a deep indent. Fill center with ½ teaspoon preserves.

6. Bake 7–8 minutes or until firm, with bottom lightly browned. Cool on wire rack.

PER SERVING

| | |
|---|---|
| Calories 65 | Total Fat 3 grams |
| Carbohydrate 9 grams | Saturated Fat .5 grams |
| Sugars 4 grams | Protein 1 gram |
| Fiber 0 grams | Sodium 75 milligrams |

Diabetic exchange = ½ Carbohydrate

WW point comparison = 2 points

# Snow-Dusted Tea Cakes

*Serves Twenty*

*Around our house the holiday season is a time for family, food, and celebration. Of course, cookies are always part of the mix. Over the years I have seen lots of recipes for cookies that are made from a mixture of ground nuts, butter, and flour, and then rolled in powdered sugar. My lovely assistant Sophia came up with the name for our version of these melt-in-your-mouth one-bite cakes as she found them the perfect companion to a nice cup of tea.*

INGREDIENTS:

¾ cup almond flour or 1 cup whole almonds

½ cup all-purpose flour

¼ cup butter, softened

¾ cup Splenda Granulated sweetener

1 large egg

½ teaspoon almond extract

1 tablespoon powdered sugar

*One way to make perfectly shaped and evenly sized cookies every time is to use a 1-tablespoon scoop, available at most kitchen stores.*

STEPS:

1. Preheat oven to 350°F. Coat a baking sheet with nonstick cooking spray.

2. If using whole almonds, place almonds in a food processor and process until very finely chopped but not powdery or oily. Pour ground almonds or almond flour into a small mixing bowl. Add all-purpose flour. Combine and set aside.

3. In a large bowl, using an electric mixer, beat butter and sweetener until mixed together (mixture will not be creamy). Add the egg and almond extract and beat until light and fluffy. Add flour mixture and gently stir until all ingredients are well blended.

4. Roll level tablespoons of dough into round balls and place 1¼ inches apart on the baking sheet. Bake 12–15 minutes, until tops are slightly browned and bottoms are golden brown.

5. Remove cookies and cool. Sift powdered sugar across tops of cookies.

**PER SERVING (1 COOKIE)**

| | |
|---|---|
| Calories 70 | Total Fat 5 grams |
| Carbohydrate 5 grams | Saturated Fat 2 grams |
| Sugars 1 gram | Protein 2 grams |
| Fiber <1 gram | Sodium 0 milligrams |

Diabetic exchange = 1 Fat, ½ Starch
WW point comparison = 1 point

# Pies, Crisps, and Cobblers

Mmm—nothing makes a home smell better than a pie in the oven. Who can resist the great aroma of a fresh-baked apple pie? Or pumpkin or peach, for that matter. In fact, when you think of good old-fashioned baking, pies often take center stage. Sadly, they are also in the spotlight when naming desserts that are high in sugar, fat, and calories. One culprit here is the crust. A traditional two-crust pie can have three hundred calories and more than 20 grams of fat in the crust alone. Of course, when you start adding sugar—and fat-laden fillings—watch out! In this chapter, you will learn the trick to making delicious pies that have only a fraction of the fat, calories, and, of course, sugar. My stepdaughter, Colleen, had the good fortune to be on spring break the week we originally tested pies. She reminded me how a great pie can welcome someone into your home. With so many types to choose from, there is always the perfect pie to do the job. From your classic fruit pies and luscious cream pies to rich-tasting no-bake versions, you'll find them all here, along with a warm apple crisp and two of my fruity non-pie favorites, Blackberry Cobbler and Cherry Berry Pandowdy. If you think about it, you can almost smell them baking.

# Single-Crust Pie Pastry
*Serves Eight*

*In order to have a great pie, you have to start with a great pie crust. This tasty version has half the fat of some homemade crusts and only one-quarter the saturated fat. After many trials, I verified that solid fats are the best choice for a tender crust. Additionally, the small amount of sugar helps to reduce gluten formation, also resulting in a more tender crust. If you are short on time, or simply prefer to use a pre-made crust, many are available. Be sure to check labels to ensure the nutritional content is comparable to this one and you'll be fine.*

INGREDIENTS:

**1 cup all-purpose flour**

**1 tablespoon cornstarch**

**2 teaspoons sugar**

**¼ teaspoon salt (scant)**

**2 tablespoons shortening**

**2 tablespoons margarine (or butter, which adds 1 gram of saturated fat)**

**2 tablespoons ice water**

**2 tablespoons cold 1% milk**

STEPS:

1. Stir together the flour, cornstarch, sugar, and salt in a medium mixing bowl. Cut in the margarine and the shortening, using either a pastry blender or fingers, until the margarine and shortening are evenly distributed in small crumbs.

2. Mix the milk and the water together and pour onto the flour mixture. Toss the pastry with a fork until it just starts to come together. Using your hands, form the pastry into a ball by gathering up all the flour mixture. (You may add a few more drops of milk or water, if necessary, to pull all the flour together.)

3. Pat the ball into a flat disk and place between two sheets of wax paper. Refrigerate for 30 minutes or longer. Roll dough from center to edge to form an 11-inch circle.

4. Remove paper and gently ease the pastry into a 9-inch pie pan. Press down on pastry to smooth. Patch as needed; turn excess under edges and crimp or flute, as desired.

Continues on next page . . .

**PER SERVING**

| | |
|---|---|
| Calories 110 | Total Fat 6 grams |
| Carbohydrate 13 grams | Saturated Fat 1.5 grams |
| Sugars 1 gram | Protein 2 grams |
| Fiber 0 grams | Sodium 70 milligrams |

Diabetic exchange = 1 Carbohydrate, 1 Fat
WW point comparison = 2½ points

5. To partially bake empty shell: Preheat oven to 425°F. Line entire shell, including edges, with aluminum foil, shiny side down, and fill foil with pie weights, rice, or dried beans. Place in bottom third of oven and bake for 10 minutes. Remove the foil and weights, prick the crust with a fork, and return to oven. Bake 10 minutes longer. If air pockets form, open oven and press down on crust with a spoon to flatten. Fill and bake according to recipe directions.

6. To fully bake empty shell: Preheat oven to 425°F. Line bottom and sides of shell with aluminum foil, shiny side down, and fill foil with pie weights, rice, or dried beans. Place in bottom third of oven and bake for 10 minutes. Remove the foil and weights, prick the crust with a fork, return to oven, and bake for 12–15 minutes more or until lightly browned. If air pockets form, open oven and press down on crust with a spoon to flatten.

*The touch of real sugar in this pie pastry helps to keep the crust tender and adds only 1 gram of sugar per serving.*

# Graham-Cracker Pie Crust

*Serves Eight*

*This pie crust is versatile and easy—and everyone loves a graham-cracker crust. I've lowered the fat by cutting back on butter and using some egg white to help bind the crust. When purchasing a pre-made graham-cracker crust, be sure to look for the low-fat version.*

INGREDIENTS:

**1 cup graham-cracker crumbs (about 16 squares)**

**2 tablespoons Splenda Granulated sweetener**

**1 tablespoon margarine or butter, melted**

**1 tablespoon canola oil**

**2 tablespoons egg white**

STEPS:

1. Preheat oven to 350°F. Lightly coat a 9-inch pie pan with nonstick cooking spray.

2. Combine crumbs in a small bowl or food processor (pulse to make crumbs from crackers).

3. Add sweetener, margarine, and oil, and stir or pulse. Add egg white and stir well, or pulse again.

4. Pour crumb mixture into pie plate. With your fingers, the back of a spoon, or with a sheet of plastic wrap, press down on the crumbs until they coat the bottom and sides of the pie plate.

5. Bake 8–10 minutes. Remove and cool.

*Butter, margarine, or oil? This recipe calls for a combination of margarine and canola oil to create a healthy and reduced-fat pie crust. You can substitute butter, with its great flavor, for all of the fat, but, of course, the saturated fat will be higher.*

PER SERVING

| | |
|---|---|
| Calories 90 | Total Fat 4.5 grams |
| Carbohydrate 12 grams | Saturated Fat 0.5 gram |
| Sugars 7 grams | Protein 1 gram |
| Fiber 0 grams | Sodium 105 milligrams |

Diabetic exchange = 1 Carbohydrate, 1 Fat
WW point comparison = 2 points

# Double Chocolate Crumb Crust

*Serves Eight*

*This is a really good crust and a definite hit with all chocoholics. On my first attempt, I simply used chocolate graham crackers instead of cookie crumbs to lower the calories and the sugar content, but I was dismayed at the loss of the deep chocolate flavor. The solution—a bit of cocoa powder to give back the rich chocolate taste, and Splenda Granulated to sweeten it up. Chocolate grahams never had it so good.*

INGREDIENTS:

**1 cup chocolate graham-cracker crumbs (about 14 squares)**

**1 tablespoon Dutch-process cocoa powder (like Hershey's Special Dark)**

**¼ cup Splenda Granulated sweetener**

**1 tablespoon margarine or butter, melted**

**1 tablespoon canola oil**

**1 large egg white (about 3 tablespoons)**

STEPS:

1. Preheat oven to 350°F. Lightly coat a 9-inch pie pan with nonstick cooking spray.

2. Combine crumbs in a small bowl or food processor (pulse to make crumbs from crackers).

3. Add cocoa powder, sweetener, margarine, and oil, and stir or pulse. Add egg white and stir well, or pulse again.

4. Pour crumb mixture into pie plate. With your fingers, the back of a spoon, or with a sheet of plastic wrap, press down on the crumbs until they coat the bottom and sides of the pie plate.

5. Bake 8–10 minutes.

**PER SERVING**

| | |
|---|---|
| Calories 90 | Total Fat 4.5 grams |
| Carbohydrate 12 grams | Saturated Fat 0.5 gram |
| Sugars 7 grams | Protein 2 grams |
| Fiber 0 grams | Sodium 95 milligrams |

Diabetic exchange = 1 Carbohydrate, 1 Fat
WW point comparison = 2 points

*If you are really watching your carbohydrates, be sure to look closely before substituting a pre-made chocolate crumb crust. I have yet to see one on the market that does not have considerably more sugar, carbs, and calories.*

# Vanilla Crumb Crust

*Serves Eight*

*Would you believe there are actually fewer calories and grams of carbohydrate in this cookie crust than an ordinary pastry crust? I use this for the Coconut and Triple Vanilla Cream Pies, and it's wonderful. It would also be delicious filled with your favorite chocolate filling.*

INGREDIENTS:

**1 generous cup crushed vanilla wafers (about 28 wafers)**

**1 tablespoon Splenda Granulated sweetener**

**2 teaspoons margarine or butter, melted**

**1 tablespoon egg white**

STEPS:

1. Preheat oven to 350°F. Lightly coat a 9-inch pie pan with nonstick cooking spray.

2. Combine crumbs in a small bowl or food processor (pulse to make crumbs from wafers). Add sweetener and margarine, and stir or pulse. Add egg white and stir well, or pulse again.

3. Pour crumb mixture into pie plate. With your fingers, the back of a spoon, or with a sheet of plastic wrap, press down on the crumbs until they coat the bottom and sides of the pie plate.

4. Bake 8-10 minutes.

*Quick tip: Put your hand in a baggie before pressing on the crumbs. The crumbs don't stick to plastic, so it's easy to get them to stick to the pan rather than your hand.*

**PER SERVING**

| | |
|---|---|
| Calories 85 | Total Fat 4.5 grams |
| Carbohydrate 10 grams | Saturated Fat 1 gram |
| Sugars 4 grams | Protein 1 gram |
| Fiber 0 grams | Sodium 60 milligrams |

Diabetic exchange = ½ Carbohydrate, 1 Fat
WW point comparison = 2 points

# Apple Pie in a Bag

*Serves Eight*

When I was growing up, we visited "apple country" every fall. The area produced a cookbook, and one of our most treasured recipes: a one-crust apple pie with a crumb topping that you actually cooked in a paper grocery bag. The bag recirculates the steam and imparts a wonderful texture to the apples and the joy of ripping it open to reveal a gorgeous pie is always amazing. I've made the pie many times with no ill effects. I mention this because the USDA now states that this cooking method may not be advisable due to chemicals and dyes in some paper bags. So, if you prefer, you may substitute a cooking bag like the ones used to roast meat.

INGREDIENTS:

**1 Single-Crust Pie Pastry, page 79, or prepared single pie crust★**

**6 medium baking apples (about 2½ pounds)**

**1 tablespoon lemon juice**

**6 tablespoons Splenda Granulated sweetener**

**1 tablespoon all-purpose flour**

**½ teaspoon cinnamon**

TOPPING

**½ cup Splenda Granulated sweetener**

**6 tablespoons all-purpose flour**

**½ teaspoon cinnamon**

**3 tablespoons margarine**

**1 Brown-and-Serve cooking bag**

**1 tablespoon all-purpose flour**

★When choosing a frozen pie crust, select one that is "deep dish."

STEPS:

1. Preheat oven to 400°F.
2. Prepare and set aside one 9-inch unbaked pie pastry shell.
3. Pare, core, and quarter apples. Halve each quarter crosswise to make chunks. Place in a large bowl and sprinkle with lemon juice.
4. Add 6 tablespoons sweetener, flour, and cinnamon and toss to coat well. Spoon coated apples into shell.
5. TOPPING: Combine ½ cup sweetener, flour, and cinnamon in a small bowl. Cut in margarine until mixture resembles coarse crumbs.
6. Sprinkle over the apples, covering entire top of pie. Place 1 tablespoon of flour into Brown-and-Serve bag and shake. Slide pie into the cooking bag and seal.
7. Place on cookie sheet and place in oven. Bake for 50 minutes or until apples are bubbly and top is browned.
8. Carefully open bag and remove pie.

**PER SERVING**

| | |
|---|---|
| Calories 210 | Total Fat 9 grams |
| Carbohydrate 30 grams | Saturated Fat 2.5 grams |
| Sugars 13 grams | Protein 2 grams |
| Fiber 2 grams | Sodium 140 milligrams |

Diabetic exchange = 1 Fruit, 1 Carbohydrate, 2 Fat
WW point comparison = 5 points

*Bakeries often sweeten no-sugar-added pies with concentrated apple juice which is the same as using sugar. Always check labels carefully—or better yet—make your own pie.*

# Pumpkin Pie

## Serves Eight

*It just wouldn't be Thanksgiving without pumpkin pie. This lightened-up version is the perfect ending to a heavy holiday meal. If you prefer your pie to have a lighter rather than custard-like texture, simply beat the egg whites and fold them in last. The Pumpkin Custard Cups on page 136 feature a variation of this same delicious filling prepared in individual soufflé or custard cups to make a delicious, creamy custard that eliminates the crust and its calories altogether.*

INGREDIENTS:

**1 Single-Crust Pie Pastry, page 79, or prepared single pie crust***

**1 large egg white beaten with 2 teaspoons water**

FILLING

**1 large egg**

**2 egg whites (or additional large egg)**

**1 15-ounce can pumpkin purée (not pie filling)**

**¾ cup Splenda Granulated sweetener**

**1 tablespoon molasses**

**2 teaspoons cornstarch**

**1½ teaspoons cinnamon**

**½ teaspoon ginger**

**¼ teaspoon allspice (optional)**

**¼ teaspoon ground cloves**

**1 teaspoon vanilla extract**

**1 12-ounce can evaporated skim milk**

*When choosing a frozen pie crust, select one that is "deep dish."

**PER SERVING**

| | |
|---|---|
| Calories 200 | Total Fat 7 grams |
| Carbohydrate 26 grams | Saturated Fat 1.5 grams |
| Sugars 9 grams | Protein 8 grams |
| Fiber 3 grams | Sodium 160 milligrams |

Diabetic exchange = 1 Carbohydrate, 1 Fat, ½ Low-Fat Milk, ½ Vegetable

WW point comparison = 4 points

STEPS:

1. Preheat oven to 425°F.

2. Prepare a partially baked crust according to directions. Remove from oven and immediately brush bottom and sides of the crust with beaten egg white and water mixture. Set aside to dry.

3. In a large bowl, whisk egg and egg whites. Add pumpkin, sweetener, molasses, cornstarch, spices, and vanilla. Mix well. Whisk in milk.

4. Pour the filling into pre-baked crust.

5. Bake at 425°F for 10 minutes. Then reduce the heat to 350°F and bake 30–35 minutes longer, or until a knife inserted near the center comes out clean. Cool pie on wire rack.

*A common problem with pumpkin pies is soggy crust. A low-fat shell only exacerbates the problem. The solution is partially baking and then sealing the crust to keep it crisp. Follow the same instructions if you choose to start with an uncooked convenience pie crust.*

# Peach Custard Pie

*Serves Eight*

*This pie is a sweet burst of summer. Fresh peaches are set into an open crust and covered with a creamy custard. There is just enough custard to hold the peaches together, letting the fresh peach taste shine through.*

INGREDIENTS:

1 Single-Crust Pie Pastry, page 79,
  or prepared pie crust

1 egg white beaten with 2 teaspoons water

1 large egg

1 tablespoon melted butter or margarine

1 tablespoon all-purpose flour

1 tablespoon cornstarch

¼ teaspoon almond extract

¼ cup nonfat half-and-half

½ cup + 2 tablespoons Splenda Granulated
  sweetener

2 pounds fresh peaches, peeled and sliced
  (8 medium peaches)

1 tablespoon all-purpose flour

1 teaspoon sugar (optional)

STEPS:

1. Preheat oven to 425°F.

2. Prepare a partially baked pie crust according to directions. Remove from oven and immediately brush bottom and sides of the crust with beaten egg white and water. Set aside.

3. In a small mixing bowl, whisk together the large egg and next 6 ingredients to make the custard. Set aside.

4. Place the peach slices in a large bowl, and toss with 2 tablespoons sweetener and 1 tablespoon flour. Place peaches into crust. You may arrange them by making circles, starting from the outside of the crust and working your way in, or you can just spoon them in randomly.

5. Pour the custard mixture over the peaches.

6. Bake at 425°F for 10 minutes. Turn oven down to 350°F and continue to bake 40 minutes longer, or until the custard appears firmly set when the pan is shaken.

7. Sprinkle 1 teaspoon of sugar for "sparkle" if desired. Let cool on a rack.

---

**PER SERVING**

| | |
|---|---|
| Calories 190 | Total Fat 9 grams |
| Carbohydrate 25 grams | Saturated Fat 2.5 grams |
| Sugars 8 grams | Protein 3 grams |
| Fiber 2 grams | Sodium 135 milligrams |

Diabetic exchange = 1 Carbohydrate, ½ Fruit, 2 Fat
WW point comparison = 4 points

*Compare this recipe to a piece of classic Peach Custard Pie, which has 398 calories, 21 grams of fat (13 saturated), 49 carbohydrate, and 26 grams of sugar.*

**Pomegranate Iced Tea (p. 33)**

**Sour Cream Chocolate
Chocolate Chip Muffins (p. 49)**

**Strawberry Banana Smoothie (p. 39),
Orange Sunshine Smoothie (p. 41)**

**Cinnamon Streusel Coffeecake (p. 57)**

Old Fashioned Peanut Butter Cookies (p. 67), Great Oatmeal Cookies (p. 65),
Better for You Chewy Chocolate Chip Cookies (p. 63)

**Apple Pie in a Bag (p. 84)**

**Cherry Berry Pandowdy (p. 95)**

Coconut Cream Pie (p. 87)

"Marvel-ous" Lemon Mousse (p. 139)

**Black and White Cheesecake "Cupcakes"** (p. 123)

Tiramisu in a Glass (p. 140)

Triple Chocolate Cheesecake (p. 122)

**Pumpkin Spice Cake (p. 104) with Whipped Cream Cheese
Topping and Frosting (p. 159)**

**Fresh Banana Cake (p. 103)**

**Blueberry Cheesecake Parfait (p. 127)**

**Red Velvet Cupcakes (p. 101)**

# Coconut Cream Pie

*Serves Eight*

*I love this dessert! I rarely eat more than a bite or two of cream pie because I know how very rich it is. A slice of traditional coconut cream pie can clock in at close to 500 calories. It took more than a trick or two to keep the luscious richness of the original, though using far less sugar and fat. I knew I had accomplished my goal when my neighbor, who has experience as a professional recipe developer, couldn't believe that this pie was not only low in fat but had only 2 tablespoons of sugar in the entire recipe.*

INGREDIENTS:

**1 Vanilla Crumb Crust, page 83**

FILLING

**¾ cup Splenda Granulated sweetener**

**¼ cup cornstarch**

**1½ cups 1% milk**

**1 cup nonfat half-and-half**

**1 large egg + 1 large egg yolk, lightly beaten**

**2 teaspoons coconut extract**

**½ teaspoon vanilla extract**

**2 tablespoons shredded coconut**

TOPPING

**1 tablespoon cornstarch**

**2 tablespoons sugar**

**⅓ cup water**

**4 large egg whites (or 6 pasteurized egg whites)**

**¼ teaspoon cream of tartar**

**½ cup Splenda Granulated sweetener**

**3 tablespoons shredded coconut**

**PER SERVING**

| | |
|---|---|
| Calories 210 | Total Fat 8 grams |
| Carbohydrate 28 grams | Saturated Fat 4 grams |
| Sugars 12 grams | Protein 6 grams |
| Fiber 0 grams | Sodium 150 milligrams |

Diabetic exchange = 2 Carbohydrate, 1 Lean Meat, 1 Fat
WW point comparison = 5 points

STEPS:

1. FILLING: In a medium saucepan, combine the sweetener and cornstarch. Stir in the milk and half-and-half; whisk until cornstarch completely dissolves. Add beaten eggs and whisk. Bring mixture to a low simmer over medium heat, stirring constantly. As the mixture starts to thicken, remove from heat briefly, and stir thoroughly, to discourage lumps. Return to heat, simmer, and stir for 1–2 minutes. Pudding should be thick and smooth.

2. Stir in extracts and coconut and remove from heat. Pour into the prepared crust and cover with plastic wrap while preparing topping.

3. Preheat oven to 400°F.

4. TOPPING: Place cornstarch and sugar in a small saucepan. Add water and stir to form a smooth, thin paste. Place over medium heat and bring to a boil. Stir and boil for 15 seconds. Cover the thick translucent paste with a lid.

Continues on next page . . .

5. In a medium (grease-free) bowl, beat egg whites until foamy. Beat in cream of tartar. Gradually beat in sweetener. Beat until stiff but not dry. Lower speed and beat in the cornstarch paste, 1 tablespoon at a time. Increase speed and beat 30 seconds.

6. Remove plastic wrap from pie and cover with meringue topping. Be sure to cover the pie all the way to the edges of the crust. Sprinkle the 3 remaining tablespoons of coconut on top.

7. Bake 10 minutes or until coconut toasts and meringue lightly browns. Remove and cool on rack. When completely cool, place in the refrigerator. The exterior of the meringue can toughen slightly after a day.

*To make a meringue, you need to stabilize the egg whites. The cornstarch/sugar paste makes this possible with only a fraction of the sugar normally used in traditional meringue recipes.*

# Triple Vanilla Cream Pie

*Serves Eight*

*You get not one, not two, but three doses of vanilla in one creamy pie. This easy-to-make cream pie really fills the bill if you enjoy vanilla. After imagining how good vanilla pudding would taste in the Vanilla Crumb Crust, I couldn't resist putting the two together. Add a vanilla-scented cream topping and you've got one delectable pie.*

INGREDIENTS:

**1 Vanilla Crumb Crust, page 83**

**1 recipe Vanilla Pudding (pie variation), page 133**

**1½ cups light whipped topping, thawed**

**½ teaspoon vanilla extract**

STEPS:

1. Prepare pudding using the pie variation.

2. Pour hot filling into pie crust. Cover surface with plastic wrap. Cool completely on rack; then refrigerate until completely chilled.

3. In a medium bowl, combine whipped topping and vanilla extract. Spread over pie. Refrigerate.

**PER SERVING**

Calories 180                          Total Fat 8 grams

Carbohydrate 22 grams          Saturated Fat 3 grams

   Sugars 8 grams                Protein 4 grams

   Fiber 0 grams                  Sodium 90 milligrams

Diabetic exchange = 1½ Carbohydrate, 1 Fat,
   ½ Lean Meat

WW point comparison = 4 points

# Chocolate Mint Cream Pie

*Serves Eight*

*One day when I was running into the grocery store for a few more testing ingredients, I happened to notice a local Girl Scout troop selling cookies. I wondered if there was anybody who didn't love those Thin Mint cookies. Just then, inspiration struck—the result was Chocolate Mint Cream Pie. Another Thin Mint fan, a lovely reader and Weight Watcher, told me she chose this pie for a gathering of her friends, and her only suggestion—you better make two!*

INGREDIENTS:

**1 Double Chocolate Crumb Crust, page 82**

FILLING

**¾ cup Splenda Granulated sweetener**

**3 tablespoons cornstarch**

**2 tablespoons Dutch-process cocoa powder (like Hershey's Special Dark)**

**½ cup nonfat half-and-half**

**1½ cups 1% milk**

**1 large egg, beaten**

**⅓ cup semisweet chocolate chips**

**1 teaspoon vanilla extract**

TOPPING

**1½ cups light whipped topping, thawed**

**2 tablespoons Splenda Granulated sweetener**

**¼ teaspoon mint extract (scant)**

STEPS:

1. FILLING: In a medium saucepan, combine the sweetener, cornstarch, and cocoa powder. Stir in the milk and half-and-half; whisk until cornstarch completely dissolves. Add the beaten egg and whisk. Bring mixture to a low simmer over medium heat, stirring constantly.

2. As the mixture starts to thicken, remove from heat briefly and stir thoroughly, including sides of the pot, to discourage lumps.

3. Add chocolate, return to heat, simmer and stir for 1–2 minutes. Pudding should be thick and smooth.

4. Add vanilla, stir, and remove from heat. Pour hot filling into pie crust. Cover surface with plastic wrap. Cool completely on rack, then refrigerate until completely chilled.

5. TOPPING: In a medium bowl, fold sweetener and mint extract into whipped topping. Spread over pie. Refrigerate.

CHOCOLATE PEPPERMINT PIE VARIATION: Substitute peppermint extract for mint.

**PER SERVING**

| | |
|---|---|
| Calories 200 | Total Fat 8 grams |
| Carbohydrate 27 grams | Saturated Fat 4 grams |
| Sugars 13 grams | Protein 5 grams |
| Fiber 1 gram | Sodium 150 milligrams |

Diabetic exchange = 2 Carbohydrate, 1 Lean Meat, 1 Fat
WW point comparison = 4 points

# Lemon Chiffon Pie

*Serves Eight*

*Luscious and yet so light, this creamy no-bake pie is a nice change from traditional lemon meringue. You actually do make meringue, but rather than placing it on top of the filling, you fold it in. I have chosen to place this pie in a graham-cracker crust, but you can use a pre-baked pastry crust if you prefer.*

INGREDIENTS:

**1 Graham-Cracker Pie Crust, page 81**

FILLING

**⅓ cup water**

**1 envelope unflavored gelatin**

**1 large egg + 2 large egg yolks, beaten (reserve whites to use below)**

**¾ cup + 3 tablespoons Splenda Granulated sweetener**

**½ cup lemon juice**

**2 teaspoons grated lemon rind**

**2 large egg whites (or 3 pasteurized egg whites)**

**¼ teaspoon cream of tartar**

**1 cup light whipped topping, thawed**

STEPS:

1. Place water in a small heavy saucepan and sprinkle gelatin on top. Let set for 3 minutes to soften gelatin.

2. Whisk in beaten eggs, ¾ cup sweetener, lemon juice, and lemon rind.

3. Stirring constantly with a wooden spoon or heatproof rubber spatula, cook over medium heat until the mixture thickens enough to coat spoon or spatula. Pour the mixture into a large bowl and refrigerate for 45–60 minutes, until mixture mounds when dropped from a spoon, but is not set.

4. In a large bowl, beat egg whites and cream of tartar until foamy. Continue to beat; gradually add remaining sweetener and beat until stiff but not dry.

5. Using a large rubber spatula or spoon, gently fold egg whites into cooled lemon mixture. Fold in whipped topping. Spoon filling into crust and refrigerate for at least 3 hours.

**PER SERVING**

| | |
|---|---|
| Calories 140 | Total Fat 6 grams |
| Carbohydrate 18 grams | Saturated Fat 2 grams |
| Sugars 9 grams | Protein 6 grams |
| Fiber 0 grams | Sodium 145 milligrams |

Diabetic exchange = 1 Carbohydrate, 1 Medium-Fat Meat
WW point comparison = 3 points

*A traditional lemon chiffon recipe has twice the fat, but that is nothing compared to the sugar. Are you ready for this? It has 59 grams of carbohydrate, 53 of them from sugar.*

# Peanut Butter Pie

*Serves Ten*

*Although a child could make this easy no-bake pie, it's definitely not just for kids. A Double Chocolate Crumb Crust is filled with a subtle, rich, and creamy peanut butter filling and topped with drizzled chocolate. This pie looks and tastes as decadent as it sounds.*

INGREDIENTS:

**1 Double Chocolate Crumb Crust, page 82**

**½ cup reduced-fat peanut butter**

**4 ounces tub-style light cream cheese**

**4 ounces fat-free cream cheese**

**½ cup Splenda Granulated sweetener**

**¼ cup 1% milk**

**½ teaspoon vanilla extract**

**1¾ cups light whipped topping, thawed**

**1 tablespoon Chocolate Fudge Sauce, page 156, or 2 teaspoons Hershey's light chocolate syrup**

STEPS:

1. In a large mixing bowl, using an electric mixer, cream the peanut butter and the cream cheeses. Add the sweetener, milk, and vanilla. Beat until smooth. Fold in whipped topping and spoon into crust.

2. Warm the fudge sauce and drizzle back and forth across the top of the pie in a decorative fashion. You don't need to warm chocolate syrup.

3. Refrigerate for at least 1 hour before serving.

*Studies show that the monounsaturated fats in peanut butter are good for your health. If you prefer even more peanut flavor, add 2 tablespoons more reduced-fat peanut butter. This increases calories by 20, and fat, carbohydrate, and protein by 1 gram each.*

**PER SERVING**

| | |
|---|---|
| Calories 210 | Total Fat 11 grams |
| Carbohydrate 20 grams | Saturated Fat 4 grams |
| Sugars 10 grams | Protein 7 grams |
| Fiber 1 gram | Sodium 300 milligrams |

Diabetic exchange = 1 Carbohydrate, 1 Medium-Fat Meat, 1 Fat

WW point comparison = 5 points

# Classic Apple Crisp

*Serves Six*

*In the autumn, when apples are plentiful and the weather turns cooler, my thoughts turn to apple crisp. With hot tender apples and crispy oat topping, apple crisp is one of life's great comfort foods. Many crisp recipes are low in fat but loaded with sugar, but this one is simply full of apples.*

INGREDIENTS:

FILLING

**2 pounds firm baking apples (about 5 medium) peeled, cored, cut into ¼-inch slices**

**2 tablespoons orange juice**

**¼ cup Splenda Granulated sweetener**

**1 tablespoon all-purpose flour**

**½ teaspoon cinnamon**

TOPPING

**½ cup all-purpose flour**

**6 tablespoons old-fashioned oats**

**½ cup Splenda Granulated sweetener**

**1 teaspoon cinnamon**

**4 tablespoons light butter**

STEPS:

1. Preheat oven to 350°F. Lightly coat an 8 × 8-inch glass baking dish with nonstick cooking spray.

2. FILLING: In a large bowl, toss the apples with the orange juice.

3. Mix sweetener, flour, and cinnamon together in a small bowl. Sprinkle over the apples and toss.

4. Place apples in the prepared pan.

5. TOPPING: In a medium bowl, mix together the flour, oats, sweetener, and cinnamon. Cut in butter with a pastry blender, fork, or fingers until mixture resembles fine crumbs. Sprinkle topping over apples.

6. Bake for 40–45 minutes, or until apples are tender and crisp is bubbling. Delicious when served warm.

*How do you make butter "light"? By whipping in water. Light butter has half the calories and fat of regular butter because it is half water. This makes it a poor choice for cookies and cakes that require a more solid fat, but a good choice here, by giving you more butter to cut in with less calories.*

**PER SERVING**

Calories 175

Carbohydrate 33 grams

   Sugars 14 grams

   Fiber 4 grams

Total Fat 4.5 grams

   Saturated Fat 2 grams

Protein 2 grams

Sodium 20 milligrams

Diabetic exchange = 1 Carbohydrate, 1 Fruit, 1 Fat

WW point comparison = 3 points

# Ultra-Quick Triple Berry Crisp

*Serves One*

*If you are looking for a terrific good-for-you dessert, look no further. In just five, yes, five short minutes you can be enjoying a delightfully warm and delicious berry crisp made with ingredients you can easily keep on hand. A quarter-cup of light, sugar-free vanilla ice cream is the ultimate healthy topper.*

INGREDIENTS:

**¾ cup frozen mixed berries**

**1 tablespoon Splenda Granulated sweetener (or 2 Splenda packets)**

**½ teaspoon cornstarch**

**1 bar (½ package) Nature Valley Oats 'n' Honey Granola Bar**

STEPS:

1. In a small microwave-safe bowl, toss berries with sweetener and cornstarch. Microwave on high for 2 minutes.

2. While berries are cooking, place granola bar in a small bag and crush into small pieces. Remove berry mix from the microwave and top with granola pieces.

3. Let set 1 minute (if you can), and enjoy.

*Frozen berries actually work best for this crisp. Choose any type of berry (or combination) you like. Using simply blackberries is one of my favorite quick crisps.*

**PER SERVING**

Calories 150

Carbohydrate 30 grams

   Sugars 22 grams

   Fiber 4 grams

Total Fat 3.5 grams

   Saturated Fat 0 grams

Protein 5 grams

Sodium 80 milligrams

Diabetic exchange = 1 Fruit, 1 Carbohydrate

WW point comparison = 2 points

# Cherry Berry Pandowdy

*Serves Six*

*A pandowdy is simply another variation of a deep-dish pie or cobbler. It was originally served for breakfast, so feel free to eat this first thing in the morning (like my son James), or serve, as we commonly do today, for dessert. This recipe is delicious when served warm and is nice topped with a dollop of light whipped topping or sugar-free vanilla ice cream.*

INGREDIENTS:

**1 single store-bought pie crust**

**2 14.5-ounce cans tart red cherries or 1 pound fresh pitted cherries**

**2 cups fresh raspberries**

**¾ cup Splenda Granulated sweetener**

**2 tablespoons cornstarch**

**¼ teaspoon almond extract**

**1 large egg white, beaten**

**2 teaspoons granulated sugar**

STEPS:

1. Preheat oven to 400°F. Coat a 9 × 9-inch glass baking dish with nonstick cooking spray.

2. In a bowl, gently toss together cherries, raspberries, sweetener, cornstarch, and almond extract. Pour into prepared baking dish.

3. On a lightly floured surface, roll the pie crust out to a 10-inch square. Using a sharp knife, trim down to a 9 × 9-inch square. Cut nine 1-inch-thick strips. Place in an alternating basketweave pattern to build a lattice crust on top of the fruit. Brush tops of pie crust with egg white and sprinkle evenly with granulated sugar.

4. Bake for 25–30 minutes, until crust is golden brown and crisp.

*Most store-bought pie crusts come two to a package. Since this recipe only calls for one, just wrap and freeze the second one until you need it. Freezing keeps it fresh longer than storing it in the refrigerator.*

**PER SERVING**

| | |
|---|---|
| Calories 150 | Total Fat 5 grams |
| Carbohydrate 26 grams | Saturated Fat 2 grams |
| Sugars 11 grams | Protein 2 grams |
| Fiber 4 grams | Sodium 105 milligrams |

Diabetic exchange = 1 Fruit, 1 Carbohydrate
WW point comparison = 3 points

# Blackberry Cobbler

*Serves Five*

*There are many versions of cobblers. At one time, it was common to find cobblers made with pie dough, but a sweet, richer type of dough is now the norm. In some recipes, you'll find the dough covers only part of the fruit, and in others, like this one, it covers all of it. But any way you make them, cobblers are a fantastic way to eat your fruit.*

INGREDIENTS:

**3 cups blackberries (if frozen, defrost only slightly)**

**¼ cup Splenda Granulated sweetener**

**1 tablespoon cornstarch**

**1 teaspoon lemon juice**

TOPPING

**¼ cup 1% milk**

**2 teaspoons lemon juice**

**1½ tablespoons butter or margarine (melted)**

**1 cup + 2 tablespoons all-purpose flour**

**2 tablespoons Splenda Granulated sweetener**

**¾ teaspoon baking powder**

**¼ teaspoon baking soda**

**1 egg white beaten with 2 teaspoons water**

**2 teaspoons sugar (optional)**

STEPS:

1. Preheat oven to 375°F. Lightly coat an 8 × 8-inch glass baking dish or a 9-inch glass pie plate with nonstick cooking spray.

2. In a large bowl, toss the berries lightly with the sweetener, cornstarch, and 1 teaspoon lemon juice. Place in baking dish.

3. TOPPING: In a small bowl, combine milk, 2 teaspoons lemon juice, and butter. Set aside.

4. In another bowl, whisk together flour, 2 tablespoons sweetener, baking powder, and baking soda. Add milk mixture and mix with a spoon just until dough comes together. Gently knead 3–4 times until soft and uniform. Dust top and bottom of the dough with a touch of flour and place on a hard surface. Roll or pat dough gently until it is the size of the top of the baking dish. Place on top of berries and brush with egg-white mixture and sprinkle with sugar, if desired. Using a knife, make 3 vents by cutting small slits in dough.

5. Bake for 40–50 minutes or until berries are bubbly and crust is brown. Let cool 15 minutes before serving.

*Substitute any fruit for the blackberries or blend fruits together. Mixed berries, peaches and blueberries, or cherries and apples are some winning combinations.*

**PER SERVING**

| | |
|---|---|
| Calories 170 | Total Fat 4.5 grams |
| Carbohydrate 29 grams | Saturated Fat 1 gram |
| Sugars 7 grams | Protein 3 grams |
| Fiber 5 grams | Sodium 190 milligrams |

Diabetic exchange = 1 Carbohydrate, ½ Fruit, 1 Fat
WW point comparison = 3 points

# Cakes for Any Occasion

Applesauce Snack Cake

Orange Sunshine Cupcakes

Red Velvet Cupcakes

Unbelievable Chocolate Cake

Fresh Banana Cake

Pumpkin Spice Cake

California Carrot Cake with Whipped
    Cream Cheese Frosting

Citrus Chiffon Cake

Lemon Soufflé Cakes

White Yogurt Cake

Flourless Almond Torte

Chocolate Almond Torte

Lemon Coconut Layer Cake

Cakes and celebrations go hand in hand. Whether it be a birthday, holiday, or just for fun, cakes always say, "Let's have a party!" The truth is, for most of us, on those few occasions, rich desserts in moderation are not a problem. But what about those of us who like to celebrate a little more often or, of course, people who are trying to watch their weight or blood sugar? How often can we afford to splurge, or how little does our piece have to be?

The answers are not often enough, and way too little. Most cakes are unfortunately too high in fat and sugar to enjoy frequently. Not anymore! By lowering the fat and all but a fraction of the sugar in these cakes, you can now create the feel of a party whenever you want.

So, whether your idea of a party is as simple as wholesome Applesauce Snack Cake after school, moist California Carrot Cake at a barbecue, classic Red Velvet Cupcakes at a birthday party, or a Chocolate Almond Torte at a celebration dinner, now you can truly have your cake and eat it, too!

# Applesauce Snack Cake

*Serves Nine*

*Not only is this Applesauce Snack Cake quick and easy to make, but my true critics—my kids—love it. I call it a snack cake because it's the perfect kind of cake for an afternoon treat. The cinnamon-and-sugar topping means no icing is required, but a spoonful of light whipped topping never hurts.*

INGREDIENTS:

¼ cup canola oil

¾ cup + 1 tablespoon Splenda Granulated sweetener

2 tablespoons molasses

1 large egg

¾ cup unsweetened applesauce

1 teaspoon vanilla extract

1½ cups all-purpose flour

1 teaspoon baking powder

¾ teaspoon baking soda

2 teaspoons cinnamon

½ teaspoon allspice

2 teaspoons sugar

½ teaspoon cinnamon

STEPS:

1. Preheat oven to 350°F. Spray an 8 × 8-inch cake pan with nonstick cooking spray.

2. In a large mixing bowl, stir together the oil, ¾ cup sweetener, molasses, egg, applesauce, and vanilla. Sift in the flour, baking powder, baking soda, 2 teaspoons cinnamon, and allspice, and stir until smooth. Spoon batter into prepared pan.

3. In a small bowl, combine the sugar, 1 tablespoon sweetener, and ½ teaspoon cinnamon for the topping. Sprinkle with a spoon evenly over the top of the cake.

4. Bake for 20 minutes or until the center of the cake springs back when lightly touched.

**PER SERVING**

| | |
|---|---|
| Calories 170 | Total Fat 7 grams |
| Carbohydrate 24 grams | Saturated Fat 0.5 gram |
| Sugars 7 grams | Protein 3 grams |
| Fiber 2 grams | Sodium 170 milligrams |

Diabetic exchange = 1½ Carbohydrate, 1 Fat
WW point comparison = 4 points

# Orange Sunshine Cupcakes
### Serves Eight

*The trickiest part about this recipe was coming up with a healthy reduced-sugar frosting. Although I've seen many reduced-fat frosting recipes, I've never found one also low in sugar. Then I remembered an icing I made as a teenager. You make a flour paste and beat it into a base of granulated sugar and shortening. Here, I lowered the fat by using light cream cheese and heightened the flavor with orange extract. Voilà, frosting with 2 tablespoons, not 2 cups, of powdered sugar.*

INGREDIENTS:

CUPCAKES

**1 cup cake flour**

**1 teaspoon baking powder**

**½ teaspoon baking soda**

**2 tablespoons margarine**

**2 tablespoons canola oil**

**⅔ cup Splenda Granulated sweetener**

**1 large egg**

**1 teaspoon vanilla extract**

**¼ cup 1% milk**

**⅓ cup regular or light orange juice**

WHIPPED FROSTING

**½ cup 1% milk**

**2 tablespoons all-purpose flour**

**2 tablespoons vegetable shortening**

**4-ounce tub-style light cream cheese**

**1 cup Splenda Granulated sweetener**

**2 tablespoons powdered sugar**

**½ teaspoon orange extract**

**PER SERVING**

| | |
|---|---|
| Calories 170 | Total Fat 9 grams |
| Carbohydrate 17 grams | Saturated Fat 3 grams |
| Sugars 4 grams | Protein 2 grams |
| Fiber 0 grams | Sodium 210 milligrams |

Diabetic exchange = 1 Carbohydrate, 2 Fat
WW point comparison = 4 points

STEPS:

1. Preheat oven to 325°F. Spray 8 muffin cups with nonstick cooking spray.

2. CUPCAKES: Sift the cake flour with the baking powder and baking soda. Set aside.

3. In a large bowl, cream the margarine and oil with an electric mixer. Add sweetener, egg, and vanilla and beat well. By hand, stir in half of flour mixture to the creamed ingredients. Add the milk and mix until smooth. Stir in the remaining flour and finish with the orange juice.

4. Spoon into the prepared pans, filling ⅔ full. Bake for 15 minutes or until cupcakes spring back when lightly touched in the center. Remove from oven and cool.

5. FROSTING: Pour milk into a small pot and add flour. Stir until smooth with no lumps. Place over low heat and cook until a smooth, thick paste forms. Set aside to cool slightly. Place shortening and cream cheese in a small mixing bowl. Beat at high speed with an electric mixer until creamy. Beat in sweetener. Add flour paste and continue to beat until smooth and creamy. Add powdered sugar and extract.

6. Frost each cooled cupcake with 1½ tablespoons of frosting. You will use most but not all of the frosting.

# Red Velvet Cupcakes

*Serves Twelve*

*A trip to a cupcake bakery was all it took to remind me of the simple glory of a red velvet cupcake. After many tries, I felt I finally got these right, so I passed them on to a recipe tester just to make sure. I was delighted to receive her note that read, "These are the best, simply the best." So now I can confidently say to you that if you've never tried red velvet cupcakes, you are in for a scrumptious treat! (And yes, you must use an entire bottle of red food coloring to give them their royal red color). To give your red velvet cupcakes the royal treatment they deserve, top them with the Whipped Cream Cheese Topping and Frosting on page 159.*

## INGREDIENTS:

**1 large egg**

**⅓ cup oil**

**¼ cup sugar**

**¾ teaspoon vanilla extract**

**¾ cup buttermilk**

**¾ cup Splenda Granulated sweetener**

**1 1-ounce bottle (or 2 tablespoons) red food coloring**

**1½ cups + 2 tablespoons cake flour**

**2 tablespoons cocoa powder**

**1 teaspoon baking powder**

**¾ teaspoon baking soda**

## STEPS:

1. Preheat oven to 350°F. Coat a nonstick 12-muffin tin with nonstick baking spray.

2. In a medium-sized mixing bowl, whisk egg until at least double in volume; mix in oil, sugar, vanilla extract, buttermilk, sweetener, and red food color.

3. Sift flour, cocoa powder, baking powder, and baking soda into wet mixture. Batter will seem a little runnier than cake mix from a box—it is supposed to be this way.

4. Scoop evenly into muffin tins and bake 15 minutes, until center springs back when touched or a toothpick comes out clean. Cool completely.

*A typical cupcake bakery red velvet cupcake with cream cheese frosting has over 500 royal calories!*

## PER SERVING (1 CUPCAKE)

| | |
|---|---|
| Calories 140 | Total Fat 6 grams |
| Carbohydrate 18 grams | Saturated Fat .5 grams |
| Sugars 5 grams | Protein 2 grams |
| Fiber 1 gram | Sodium 140 milligrams |

Diabetic exchange = 1 Carbohydrate, 1 Fat
WW point comparison = 2 points

# Unbelievable Chocolate Cake

*Serves Nine*

*A chocolate cake that takes only one bowl, a whisk, and 10 minutes to make and contains only ¼ cup of sugar is, well, pretty unbelievable! I've also received three great ideas from readers who doubled this recipe: 1) Bake in a 9 × 13-inch pan for 28–30 minutes for a sheet cake; 2) Bake in two 9-inch rounds for a layer cake; 3) Split the rounds in half and fill with the Whipped Cream Cheese Topping and Frosting (page 159) for a torte. I really enjoy this cake dusted with powdered sugar and served with sliced strawberries.*

## INGREDIENTS:

¼ cup canola oil

1 large egg

1 teaspoon vanilla extract

¼ cup brown sugar, packed (use fresh brown sugar, with no hard lumps)

1 cup Splenda Granulated sweetener

1 cup low-fat buttermilk

1¼ cups cake flour

1 teaspoon baking powder

1 teaspoon baking soda

¼ cup Dutch-process cocoa powder (like Hershey's Special Dark)

¼ cup hot water

2 teaspoons powdered sugar

Easy Chocolate Cream Frosting, page 160 (optional)

## STEPS:

1. Preheat oven to 350°F. Spray an 8 × 8-inch★ baking pan with nonstick cooking spray.

2. In a large bowl, whisk together the oil and the egg for 1 minute until the mixture is thick and frothy. Add the vanilla, brown sugar, and sweetener, and beat with a whisk for 2 more minutes until the mixture is thick and smooth and the sugars have been thoroughly beaten into the mixture. Add 1 cup buttermilk and mix.

3. Using a sifter or a metal sieve, sift the flour, baking powder, baking soda, and cocoa powder into the liquid mixture. Whisk vigorously for 1–2 minutes until the batter is nice and smooth. Pour the hot water into the batter and whisk one more time until the batter is again nice and smooth. The batter will be thin.

4. Pour the batter into the prepared cake pan and tap the pan on the counter to level the surface and to help remove any air bubbles.

5. Bake for 18–20 minutes or just until the center springs back when touched and a cake tester or toothpick comes out clean. Do not overcook. Remove the cake from the oven and cool.

6. Before serving, dust with powdered sugar or frost with Chocolate Cream Frosting.

★ Be careful not to substitute a 9-inch square pan; if you need to substitute, use a 9-inch round pan.

## PER SERVING

| | |
|---|---|
| Calories 160 | Total Fat 7 grams |
| Carbohydrate 22 grams | Saturated Fat 1 gram |
|    Sugars 8 grams | Protein 3 grams |
|    Fiber 1 gram | Sodium 200 milligrams |

Diabetic exchange = 1½ Carbohydrate, 1 Fat

WW point comparison = 4 points

# Fresh Banana Cake

*Serves Eight*

*Every time I have some overripe bananas, I think of this cake. The recipe is easy and practically foolproof. I have made it many times (as have my friends and my friends' friends). I have also made it with and without sugar and am happy to report it is just as wonderful without it. Lastly, this cake's so moist that you'll find it hard to believe it's so low in fat.*

INGREDIENTS:

3 small bananas, mashed (about
  1 cup purée)

2 tablespoons canola oil

⅔ cup Splenda Granulated sweetener

1 tablespoon molasses (or honey)

1 large egg

1 large egg white

½ cup nonfat plain yogurt

2 teaspoons vanilla extract

1½ cups cake flour

1 teaspoon baking powder

¾ teaspoon baking soda

2 teaspoons powdered sugar (optional)

STEPS:

1. Preheat oven to 350°F. Spray a 9-inch cake pan with nonstick cooking spray.

2. Place banana purée in a large mixing bowl. Whisk in next 7 ingredients (oil through vanilla).

3. Sift cake flour, baking powder, and baking soda into the bowl. Stir to blend in dry ingredients.

4. Spoon batter into prepared pan. Bake for 30 minutes or until a toothpick inserted into the center of the cake comes out clean. Cool in pan on wire rack.

5. Sift powdered sugar over cake just prior to serving if desired.

*This is a great old-fashioned homestyle cake. When serving it to guests, I warm it up and then top each piece with a spoonful of light whipped topping and a few slices of fresh banana.*

PER SERVING

| | |
|---|---|
| Calories 130 | Total Fat 3.5 grams |
| Carbohydrate 21 grams | Saturated Fat 0 grams |
| Sugars 7 grams | Protein 3 grams |
| Fiber 1 gram | Sodium 300 milligrams |

Diabetic exchange = 1½ Carbohydrate, ½ Fat
WW point comparison = 3 points

# Pumpkin Spice Cake

*Serves Eight*

*A favorite around our house, especially during the holidays, this moist and tasty cake is very simple to make and a guaranteed crowd pleaser. An easy way to serve this spice cake is to finish it off with a light dusting of powdered sugar, but for the holidays I recommend a more decadent approach. The Whipped Cream Cheese Frosting on page 159 is always a hit.*

INGREDIENTS:

**1 large egg**

**2 large egg whites**

**3 tablespoons dark brown sugar, packed**

**½ cup Splenda Granulated sweetener**

**¾ cup pumpkin purée**

**3 tablespoons each canola oil and applesauce**

**1¼ cups cake flour**

**¾ teaspoon baking soda**

**¾ teaspoon baking powder**

**1½ teaspoons ground cinnamon**

**½ teaspoon ground ginger**

**¼ teaspoon ground nutmeg**

**⅛ teaspoon ground cloves**

STEPS:

1. Preheat oven to 350°F. Coat an 8-inch round baking pan with nonstick baking spray.

2. In a large mixing bowl, with an electric mixer on high, beat together eggs, brown sugar, and sweetener for 3–4 minutes or until tripled in volume. With a large wooden spoon or spatula, mix in pumpkin, oil, and applesauce.

3. Place a fine mesh strainer on top of bowl and pour remaining ingredients into strainer, sifting them into the bowl. Stir to combine. Do not overmix.

4. Spoon batter into prepared baking pan and bake for 20–25 minutes, or until center springs back when lightly touched or a toothpick comes out clean.

*My favorite variation is to add ¼ cup of toasted pecans. To toast them, lay them flat on a baking sheet and bake at 400 for 5–7 minutes. Cool and chop before adding to the batter.*

---

**PER SERVING**

| | |
|---|---|
| Calories 200 | Total Fat 10 grams |
| Carbohydrate 24 grams | Saturated Fat 1 gram |
| Sugars 8 grams | Protein 4 grams |
| Fiber 2 grams | Sodium 480 milligrams |

Diabetic exchange = 1½ Carbohydrate, 2 Fat
WW point comparison = 4 points

# California Carrot Cake with Cream Cheese Frosting

*Serves Fifteen*

*I remember my mom making this popular cake when I was a child. I'm sure she thought it was nice that such a delicious treat was also good for us. What she didn't realize is that her famed carrot cake—made with lots of oil and sugar—was loaded with fat and calories. I am so happy I was able to make a Carrot Cake that retains the same moist, sweet quality of the original with so much less sugar. When topped with its delicious cream cheese frosting, this cake is guaranteed to please.*

## INGREDIENTS:

**1 cup all-purpose flour**

**1 cup wheat or white whole-wheat flour**

**2 teaspoons baking soda**

**1 teaspoon baking powder**

**2 teaspoons cinnamon**

**½ teaspoon nutmeg**

**¼ teaspoon cloves**

**⅓ cup chopped nuts**

**¼ cup prune purée/baby food prunes**

**¼ cup canola oil**

**1 teaspoon vanilla extract**

**1 large egg**

**3 large egg whites**

**⅔ cup low-fat buttermilk**

**1½ cups Splenda Granulated sweetener**

**8 ounces crushed pineapple, packed in unsweetened juice**

**1½ cups carrots, peeled and shredded**

**Whipped Cream Cheese Frosting, page 159**

## STEPS:

1. Preheat oven to 350°F. Coat a 9 × 13-inch cake pan with nonstick cooking spray.

2. In a medium bowl, combine the flours, baking soda, baking powder, spices, and chopped nuts. Stir to blend.

3. In a large bowl, measure the prune purée, oil, vanilla, and eggs. Whisk together. Add the buttermilk and sweetener. Whisk. Stir in the pineapple (including juice) and carrots. Add the flour mixture. Stir to form batter.

4. Transfer the batter into prepared pan.

5. Bake for 25–30 minutes or until a toothpick inserted in the center of the cake comes out clean. Let the cake cool in the pan on wire rack.

6. Prepare frosting according to recipe. Frost cake and serve or refrigerate.

**PER SERVING**

| | |
|---|---|
| Calories 200 | Total Fat 9 grams |
| Carbohydrate 24 grams | Saturated Fat 3 grams |
| Sugars 6 grams | Protein 7 grams |
| Fiber 2 grams | Sodium 300 milligrams |

Diabetic exchange = 1 Carbohydrate, ½ Fruit, 2 Fat
WW point comparison = 4 points

*Most carrot cakes, low in fat or not, are very high in sugar. Because they can have as much as 75 grams of carbohydrate apiece (more than a meal's worth of carbs for many persons with diabetes), they are off limits to lots of folks. This carrot cake, even with its ample pieces, actually allows you to have your cake—and dinner, too! Enjoy.*

# Citrus Chiffon Cake

*Serves Fourteen*

*A chiffon cake is a terrific cake made from a cake-like batter and lightened with egg whites. It's technically in a class of cakes called foam cakes. Like its cousin the angel food cake, the light chiffon cake is moist and often served with fresh fruit or fruit sauces. It slices and freezes well, which adds to its versatility as a great cake for entertaining.*

INGREDIENTS:

2¼ cups cake flour

1 tablespoon baking powder

½ teaspoon salt

1 cup Splenda Granulated sweetener

3 egg yolks

⅓ cup canola oil

¾ cup light orange juice

Zest of 1 orange

Zest of 1 lemon

8 egg whites

¼ cup granulated sugar

½ teaspoon cream of tartar

STEPS:

1. Preheat oven to 325°F. Set aside one 10-inch ungreased tube pan with a removable bottom (an angel food cake pan).

2. Sift together the cake flour, baking powder, and salt. Stir in the sweetener. Set aside.

3. In a large bowl, beat the yolks, oil, orange juice, and zest with an electric mixer at high speed until smooth. Incorporate the flour mixture on low speed.

4. In a separate, large, grease-free bowl, whip the egg whites, sugar, and cream of tartar until soft peaks form. Fold ¼ of the egg whites into the batter. Carefully fold in the remaining whites.

5. Spoon the batter into the pan and smooth.

6. Bake for 45–50 minutes or until the top springs back when lightly pressed. Let cool upside down on a wire rack at least 1½ hours.

*This is a new and improved version of this recipe. A kind reader wrote and told me she liked it so much that she thought it would make a good wedding cake, but every time she tried baking it in a larger, flatter pan, it fell. I have now adjusted the recipe for more stability and lift by beating some sugar into the whites. Better still, by switching to light orange juice, I've made sure that the total carbohydrates only increase 2 grams for this better-than-ever Citrus Chiffon Cake.*

**PER SERVING**

| | |
|---|---|
| Calories 145 | Total Fat 6 grams |
| Carbohydrate 18 grams | Saturated Fat 5 grams |
|    Sugars 2 grams | Protein 4 grams |
|    Fiber 0 grams | Sodium 140 milligrams |

Diabetic exchange = 1 Carbohydrate, 1 Fat

WW point comparison = 3 points

# Lemon Soufflé Cakes

*Serves Four*

*These really should be called "mistake cakes." I was trying to develop a lemon pudding cake and what came out of the oven was a cake, but there was no pudding. I thought I had a loss until I tasted the cake. Yum. It was very tasty and had a moist but airy texture. So I tried the recipe again, using 6-ounce ramekins to produce individual cakes. They were a hit. You can get the ramekins ready ahead of time and pop them in the oven while you eat. Serve them with a touch of light whipped topping and blueberries for a spectacular finish.*

## INGREDIENTS:

4 large egg whites

¾ cup + 3 tablespoons Splenda Granulated sweetener

1 tablespoon granulated sugar

2 large egg yolks

1 tablespoon butter or margarine, softened

¾ cup low-fat buttermilk

¼ cup lemon juice

1 tablespoon lemon zest

¼ cup all-purpose flour

1 teaspoon cornstarch

¼ teaspoon baking powder

2 teaspoons granulated sugar

## PER SERVING

| | |
|---|---|
| Calories 160 | Total Fat 5 grams |
| Carbohydrate 20 grams | Saturated Fat 2 grams |
|    Sugars 8 grams | Protein 7 grams |
|    Fiber 0 grams | Sodium 130 milligrams |

Diabetic exchange = 1½ Carbohydrate,
  1 Medium-Fat Meat

WW point comparison = 4 points

## STEPS:

1. Preheat oven to 350°F. Spray four 6-ounce ramekins or soufflé cups with nonstick cooking spray and place them in a larger baking pan that is at least 2 inches deep; set aside.

2. In a deep bowl, beat egg whites with an electric mixer on high speed until foamy. Beat in the 3 tablespoons sweetener and 1 tablespoon of granulated sugar until soft peaks form when beaters are lifted from the whites.

3. In another bowl, combine egg yolks, butter, and remaining sweetener and beat until thick and creamy. Stir in the next 6 ingredients (buttermilk through baking powder) and beat until smooth. Fold in one quarter of the egg whites; stir to incorporate. Gently fold in remaining egg whites.

4. Divide the batter into the ramekins (¾ full).

5. Sprinkle ½ teaspoon of granulated sugar on top of each cake.

6. Place baking dish on middle rack of the oven. Pour boiling water into the larger pan until the water reaches halfway up the ramekins. Bake for 25–30 minutes or until center feels firm to the touch. They are done as soon as the center sets.

# White Yogurt Cake

*Serves Eight*

*When I first started teaching the principles of healthy cooking, not many chefs agreed that low-fat cooking could be synonymous with great food. A decade later, many highly respected chefs have adopted the idea that healthy cooking techniques can indeed produce good food. One of those chefs is the world-renowned Jacques Pepin, whose own healthy cookbook, Simple and Healthy Cooking, inspired me to produce this Yogurt Cake. It is a basic moist white cake.*

INGREDIENTS:

1 cup + 2 tablespoons cake flour

1½ teaspoons baking powder

¼ teaspoon baking soda

3 large egg whites

3 tablespoons granulated sugar

3 tablespoons canola oil

⅔ cup Splenda Granulated sweetener

1 teaspoon vanilla extract

¼ teaspoon almond extract

1 large egg

½ cup plain nonfat yogurt

⅓ cup unsweetened applesauce

STEPS:

1. Preheat oven to 350°F. Spray an 8-inch round cake pan with nonstick cooking spray.

2. Sift the flour with the baking powder and baking soda and set aside.

3. In a medium bowl, beat egg whites until frothy. Gradually add the 3 tablespoons of sugar; continue to beat until soft peaks form when the mixer is lifted from the whites. Set aside.

4. In a large bowl, cream the oil and the sweetener. Add the next 5 ingredients (vanilla through applesauce) and beat for 1–2 minutes. (It may not look totally creamy.)

5. Add the flour sifted with the baking powder and soda to the bowl. Beat until smooth. Gently fold in the beaten egg whites.

6. Spoon the batter into the prepared pan. Bake for 20 minutes or until center of the cake springs back when lightly touched. Cool in pan on rack.

*Yogurt is a wonderful baking ingredient in everything from cakes and pies to muffins and biscuits. Its thickness helps batters hold their structure and its acid content helps both rise and tenderness. When you substitute yogurt in recipes, use a bit of baking soda (½ teaspoon per cup of yogurt).*

**PER SERVING**

| | |
|---|---|
| Calories 150 | Total Fat 6 grams |
| Carbohydrate 16 grams | Saturated Fat 0.5 gram |
| Sugars 5 grams | Protein 4 grams |
| Fiber 0 grams | Sodium 190 milligrams |

Diabetic exchange = 1 Carbohydrate, 1 Fat

WW point comparison = 4 points

# Flourless Almond Torte

*Serves Eight*

*This simple flourless torte makes for a very fancy dessert that you will love to serve on any special occasion, yet it is very simple to make. The ground blanched almonds not only give this torte that luscious, nutty macaroon flavor and texture we usually associate only with fine European pastries, they also replace the usual flour, making it quite low in carbohydrates and higher in healthy fats. The perfect accompaniments are a handful of fresh berries and a touch of light whipped topping.*

INGREDIENTS:

1¾ cups sliced blanched almonds, divided

½ cup confectioner's sugar, divided

½ cup Splenda Granulated sweetener

4 large egg whites

¼ teaspoon salt

½ teaspoon almond extract

*Although high in fat, almonds are very good for you—and your heart. Stick to eating no more than a handful a day to keep the calories in check.*

STEPS:

1. Preheat oven to 325°F. Cut a piece of wax paper or parchment paper to fit the bottom of an 8-inch round cake pan. Coat the pan with nonstick baking spray and place the prepared paper on the bottom of the pan. Spray again (on top of the paper), and sprinkle evenly with ¼ cup of the almonds.

2. Place the remaining almonds, ¼ cup of the confectioner's sugar, and sweetener into the bowl of a food processor. Process until nuts are until finely ground. Set aside.

3. In a medium bowl, using an electric mixer, beat egg whites with salt until soft peaks form. Gradually add remaining ¼ cup of confectioner's sugar until stiff glossy peaks form. Add almond extract.

4. With a large spatula, gently fold in the ground almond mixture. Evenly spread the batter into the prepared pan. Bake for 30–35 minutes until golden brown and firm in the center. Cool slightly before inverting cake onto a serving plate and removing the wax or parchment paper.

**PER SERVING**

Calories 160

Carbohydrate 12 grams

   Sugars 7 grams

   Fiber 2 grams

Total Fat 10 grams

   Saturated Fat 1 gram

Protein 6 grams

Sodium 100 milligrams

Diabetic exchange = 1 Carbohydrate, 1 Low-Fat Meat, 1 Fat

WW point comparison = 4 points

# Chocolate Almond Torte

*Serves Eight*

*In Austria and Germany, the word "torte" refers to any round cake. Here, the term torte is often reserved for cakes with many layers, or cakes that use ground nuts or bread crumbs in place of some or most of the flour. This torte uses ground almonds and very little flour to create a very dense and moist chocolate cake. Serve it dusted with powdered sugar, or with Quick Raspberry Sauce (page 154) for an elegant dessert. I like to warm the cake before placing each slice on a plate pooled with the raspberry sauce and then top it with light whipped topping.*

### INGREDIENTS:

½ **cup almonds, toasted**

¼ **cup all-purpose flour**

½ **cup + ⅓ cup Splenda Granulated sweetener**

2 **tablespoons cocoa powder**

¼ **teaspoon baking powder**

¾ **cup semisweet chocolate chips**

3 **tablespoons hot water**

⅓ **cup prune purée**

½ **teaspoon almond extract**

5 **egg whites**

½ **teaspoon cream of tartar**

2 **teaspoons powdered sugar (optional)**

### STEPS:

1. Preheat oven to 375°F. Spray bottom of an 8-inch round springform or cake pan with nonstick cooking spray.

2. Toast almonds by placing on a pie plate and baking for 5 minutes. Using a food processor, grind nuts until almost as fine as flour. Pulse in flour, ½ cup sweetener, cocoa powder, and baking powder. Set aside.

3. Melt chocolate in a small pan over hot water or place in a bowl and microwave for 1½ minutes. Stir until all chips are melted and then stir in hot water, prune purée, and almond extract. Mix flour mixture into the chocolate (it will be thick).

4. In a separate bowl, beat egg whites and cream of tartar until frothy. Gradually add ⅓ cup of sweetener and beat until soft peaks form. Fold ⅓ of egg whites into cool chocolate mixture to lighten mixture. Gently fold in remaining whites.

5. Spoon mixture into prepared pan and smooth.

6. Bake for 20–22 minutes until center is just set. Do not overbake. Let cool in pan on wire rack for at least 30 minutes.

### PER SERVING

| | |
|---|---|
| Calories 190 | Total Fat 9 grams |
| Carbohydrate 24 | Saturated Fat 2.5 grams |
| Sugars 10 grams | Protein 4 grams |
| Fiber 3 grams | Sodium 50 milligrams |

Diabetic exchange = 1½ Carbohydrate, 2 Fat
WW point comparison = 4 points

# Lemon Coconut Layer Cake

## Serves Eight

*Here's a birthday cake for those (like me!) who love lemon desserts. You split a simple white layer cake, then fill and frost it with a sumptuous lemon cream frosting. You can prepare the lemon curd far in advance of the cake and frosting, which makes putting this together a snap. I found it held very well in the refrigerator for several days.*

INGREDIENTS:

**3 egg whites**

**2 tablespoons granulated sugar**

**3 tablespoons canola oil**

**1 teaspoon vanilla extract**

**½ cup low-fat buttermilk**

**⅔ cup Splenda Granulated sweetener**

**1 large egg**

**1 cup + 2 tablespoons cake flour**

**2 teaspoons baking powder**

**¼ teaspoon baking soda**

**½ cup Lemon Curd, page 157**

**1¼ cups light whipped topping**

**⅓ cup shredded coconut**

STEPS:

1. Preheat oven to 350°F. Spray an 8-inch cake pan with nonstick cooking spray or line pan bottom with wax paper.

2. In a medium bowl, beat egg whites until frothy. Gradually add sugar and continue to beat until soft peaks form when the mixer is lifted from the whites. Set aside.

3. On medium speed, mix oil, vanilla, buttermilk, sweetener, and egg in a large bowl.

4. Sift together the cake flour, baking powder, and baking soda into the bowl and blend until smooth. Gently fold in the beaten egg whites.

5. Spoon into prepared pan and smooth top.

6. Bake for 20 minutes or until the center springs back when lightly touched. Cool cake in pan on rack for 10 minutes. Loosen cake from pan by inverting briefly. Let cake layer cool completely.

7. Set cake on plate and slice in half horizontally to make two layers.

8. Mix the Lemon Curd and the whipped topping together in a bowl. Place ½ cup of frosting on the first layer of the cake. Place second layer on top and frost top and sides with the remaining frosting. Sprinkle coconut over the top of the cake.

9. Refrigerate until time to serve.

**PER SERVING**

| | |
|---|---|
| Calories 175 | Total Fat 8 grams |
| Carbohydrate 22 grams | Saturated Fat 1.5 grams |
| Sugars 7 grams | Protein 4 grams |
| Fiber 0 grams | Sodium 200 milligrams |

Diabetic exchange = 1½ Carbohydrate, 1½ Fat
WW point comparison = 4 points

# Cheesecakes to Die For

Nothing is as rich and creamy and satisfying as a piece of cheesecake. It's no wonder that entire books—entire restaurants—have been fashioned after this indulgent dessert.

But cheesecake isn't really cake at all.

Cheesecakes are technically custards, albeit very rich custards. Baked cheesecakes, like custards, depend on eggs to help the ingredients "set." With cheesecakes, however, the main ingredient (most often cream cheese) firms up enough to be sliced like a cake—hence, the name. The problem with using cheese as a main ingredient in a cake is when you're watching your intake of fat and calories. The fact is, a single piece of cheesecake can easily have more than 50 grams of fat and 600 calories—whoa. The good news is that there are lots of ways to produce creamy, sweet cheesecakes with far less fat and a fraction—if any—of the sugar.

This section of the book is devoted to cheesecakes, cheesecakes, and even more cheesecakes. Cheesecakes for every day and cheescakes for special occasions. Cheesecakes for holidays and cheesecakes for parties. Cheesecakes with fruit and cheesecakes with chocolate! Cheesecakes in cups and cheesecake in glasses. Cheesecakes you bake and cheesecakes you don't. You will even find cheesecake for breakfast! What you won't find are cheesecakes that are difficult to make—because cheesecake is easy. And to make the perfect cheesecake every time, here are a few tips:

» You may bake cheesecakes in a regular cake pan instead of a springform pan if you don't need to present the cake whole. This means you don't have to wrap the pan when you use the water bath.

» Make sure your cheeses are at room temperature before beating. To prevent lumps, beat them until they are very smooth before adding any liquid ingredients.

» Purée cottage cheese (when specified) until it is completely smooth. This means it should be creamy and have no visible curds left.

» Add eggs last and beat them in just until blended to help avoid cracks in the finished cheesecake.

» The best way to wrap a pan for a water bath is to use a single sheet of heavy-duty aluminum foil. This way there are no seams to allow for water seepage. Set pan on foil, pull up all sides, and tightly secure at the top rim of the pan.

» For water baths, place the pan with the cheesecake mixture into the baking pan—and into the oven—before adding the hot water.

» Cheesecakes are "done" and should be removed from the oven when the center is barely set. Remember, the center should still move slightly because cheesecakes continue to set for hours after baking.

» Cheesecakes should be left in the oven to cool for the first 30 minutes (with the door open) to avoid abrupt temperature changes that can create cracks.

» Not all cracks can be avoided (especially in low-fat, low-sugar cakes), but all can be camouflaged with sweetened sour cream, fruit toppings, or light whipped topping.

# Cheesecakes 101

A cheesecake isn't really a cake at all; it's a custard. Like custard, baked cheesecakes rely on eggs, which set into a solid gel when cooked. This creates a "cake" firm enough to slice. Because this cake is made from cream cheese and other dairy products, rather than flour, it has a silky, smooth texture.

## Comparing Cheesecakes (¹⁄₁₂ of a 9-inch cheesecake)

| Cheesecake | Calories | Fat Grams | Saturated Fat Grams | Carbohydrate Grams | Sugar Grams | Protein Grams |
|---|---|---|---|---|---|---|
| Regular Cheesecake | 560 | 40 | 23 | 40 | 34 | 9 |
| Reduced-Fat Cheesecake | 420 | 23 | 14 | 44 | 36 | 10 |
| Heavenly Cheesecake (page 118) | 180 | 8 | 5 | 15 | 7 | 11 |

The number-one culprit for fat and calories in cheesecake is cream cheese. It contains nearly 800 calories and 80 grams of fat (50 of it saturated) per 8-ounce package. A single cheesecake can call for three or more packages. Additional high fat, saturated fat, and calorie contributors are full-fat sour cream and eggs. Sugar is fat-free but contains 775 calories and 200 grams of carbohydrate per cup.

» A cheesecake made entirely from *reduced fat* products has one-third less fat and fewer calories—and can taste great. Unfortunately, this version still contains over 400 calories and 23 grams of fat per serving. It also contains a whopping 36 grams—or the equivalent of 8 teaspoons—of sugar per slice!

» A cheesecake made entirely from *non-fat* products tastes non-fat and does not have the mouthfeel of regular cheesecake.

» A blend of creamed low-fat cottage cheese, low-fat cream cheese, and non-fat cream cheese in cheesecakes (to replace 24 ounces of full-fat cream cheese), gives wonderful texture and flavor with two-thirds fewer calories and 20 percent of the fat! Sugar is no longer an issue if you use Splenda Granulated sweetener—and it works great.

» Everyone that has made cheesecakes knows about cracks. They are the annoying earthquake lines (or so it seems) that can form on the top of the cake. The major causes of cracks include excessive oven temperatures, overcooking, and overbeating the batter. Cracks may be covered with fruit, fruit toppings, or sweetened sour cream.

## Cooking Tips

Cheesecakes are the perfect party dessert. They are easy to make, everybody loves them, and they are actually better if they are made a day or two in advance. The following tips, including two different ways to cook your cheesecake, will help you produce a perfect cheesecake every time.

### Pans

Springform pans are used to bake cheesecakes to allow the entire cake to be easily removed from the pan for serving. You may substitute a regular cake pan to bake the cake with no ill effects.

## Creaming Cottage Cheese

To cream the cottage cheese, place in a food processor and blender and purée on high speed. It is finished when there are *no* curds left. It will look smooth. The chefs I've taught love this trick and have used this as a replacement for mayonnaise and/or sour cream.

## Cream Cheese

Have the cream cheeses at room temperature before beating. Do not add the eggs or any liquid until the cheeses are beaten together and are smooth. If eggs or liquid are added too soon, cream cheese can form into lumps that will not smooth out. The cheesecake will still taste terrific but the lumps may show.

## Beating

Do not overbeat the batter. It can contribute to cracking. It is especially important to stop beating after the eggs have been incorporated into the batter.

## Cooking in a Water Bath

The water bath cooking method is the best insurance against cracking. It controls excessive heat and produces a cheesecake that is uniformly creamy from edge to center. When baking the cake in a springform pan, you must first seal the pan so that water will not seep into the cake. Set the pan on several sheets of aluminum foil (or one sheet if heavy duty) and fold the foil up the sides of the pan, securing at the top rim. Place the foil-wrapped unbaked cheesecake in a baking pan that is at least 3 inches wider than the cheesecake pan (a roasting dish works great). Set the roasting or baking pan on the preheated oven rack. Carefully pour very hot or boiling water halfway up the outside of the cheesecake pan. Gently slide the oven rack into the oven and bake for as long as directed. Cheesecakes cooked in regular cake pans do not need to be wrapped in foil.

## Cooking the "Traditional" Way

The traditional cooking method bakes the cheesecake at a temperature that is low enough to encourage even heating (300 to 325 degrees). For this method to work without producing cracks, you must be extremely careful not to overbeat the batter or overcook the cheesecake. In addition, you must cool the cake slowly. If you want the edges of your cheesecake to be dryer and denser than the creamy center, this is the method for you. When the cheesecake is ready to be baked, simply place in the center of the oven.

## Cooking Time

With either method, you need to know when the cheesecake is done. When finished, the cheesecake should appear firm around the edges, but the very center should still jiggle slightly when the pan is shook. Cheesecakes do not completely set until cooled.

## Cooling

The best way to cool cheesecakes is to leave them in the oven for 30 to 60 minutes after baking. Turn off the oven and prop the door open to slowly reduce the oven temperature. This ensures the cheesecake is not "shocked" by the temperature change, which can result in cracking.

# Cheesecake Crumb Crust

*Serves Twelve*

*This crumb crust is very similar to the one I use for pies. However, because cheesecakes do not require a crust on the sides, you can use fewer crumbs. Cheesecake fillings also tend to seep into the crust and help to bind it together, which eliminates the need for some of the fat and the egg white used in graham-cracker pie crusts. In order to keep the fillings from seeping too much and creating a soggy crust, I like to bake the crust separately before filling.*

INGREDIENTS:

¾ **cup graham-cracker crumbs (about 12 squares)**

**2 tablespoons Splenda Granulated sweetener**

**1 tablespoon margarine or butter, melted**

*These two basic crusts can be found on many of the cheesecakes, but other low-fat cookies such as gingersnaps and vanilla wafers can also be used, as found in the Pumpkin Streusel Cheesecake. Have some fun by mixing and matching fillings and crusts to suit your taste.*

STEPS:

1. Preheat oven to 325°F. Spray an 8- or 9-inch springform pan, as specified in cheesecake recipe, with nonstick cooking spray.

2. If starting with whole graham crackers, place them in a blender or food processor and pulse to make fine crumbs.

3. Place the crumbs in a bowl and add sweetener and melted butter or margarine. Stir to mix. Pour the crumb mixture into the bottom of the prepared pan. With your fingers, the back of a spoon, or a sheet of plastic wrap, press down on the crumbs to cover the bottom of the pan.

4. Bake for 8 minutes. Cool. (Be sure the crust is completely cool when using for unbaked cheesecakes.)

CHOCOLATE CRUMB CRUST VARIATION:
Substitute chocolate graham crackers for the regular grahams. Add 2 teaspoons cocoa powder, along with the 1 additional tablespoon sweetener and butter or margarine, to the crumbs.

**PER SERVING**

| | |
|---|---|
| Calories 40 | Total Fat 1.5 grams |
| Carbohydrate 6 grams | Saturated Fat 0.5 gram |
| Sugars 3 grams | Protein 0 grams |
| Fiber 0 grams | Sodium 55 milligrams |

Diabetic exchange = ½ Carbohydrate
WW point comparison = 1 point

# Heavenly Cheesecake

*Serves Twelve*

*This was the cheesecake in my family that was made only for special occasions. So, I really wanted my makeover to work on this one—and it did! As luck would have it, a good friend and her husband happened to be coming over for dinner so I served it for dessert. That was when my friend exclaimed, "This is my cheesecake!" And she was sure this was hers. In fact, our original recipes were almost identical. The real surprise came when she found out that my lightened version had a third of the calories, less than half the carbohydrate, and one-fifth the fat of our original recipes. Now that's "heavenly."*

INGREDIENTS:

1 8- or 9-inch baked Cheesecake
   Crumb Crust, page 117

1 cup low-fat cottage cheese

8 ounces tub-style light cream cheese

8 ounces nonfat cream cheese, room
   temperature

1¼ cups Splenda Granulated sweetener

2 tablespoons all-purpose flour

2 tablespoons cornstarch

1 teaspoon vanilla extract

½ teaspoon almond extract

1 large egg

3 large egg whites

1¼ cups light sour cream

*This is divine when topped with my Super Simple Cherry Topping (page 155).*

PER SERVING

| | |
|---|---|
| Calories 180 | Total Fat 8 grams |
| Carbohydrate 15 grams | Saturated Fat 5 grams |
| Sugars 15 grams | Protein 11 grams |
| Fiber 0 grams | Sodium 350 milligrams |

Diabetic exchange = 1 Carbohydrate, 1½ Lean Meat
WW point comparison = 4 points

STEPS:

1. Preheat oven to 325°F. Wrap any 8-inch (or 9-inch) springform pan filled with crust tightly in heavy-duty foil to make waterproof.

2. Place cottage cheese into a food processor or blender. Purée until completely smooth. Spoon into a large mixing bowl and add nonfat and light cream cheeses. Using an electric mixer, beat on medium speed until creamy. Add the sweetener, flour, cornstarch, and extracts, and beat on low until smooth. Add large egg and then egg whites, beating just briefly after each addition to incorporate. Stir in the sour cream with a large spoon. Pour into the prepared crust and smooth top.

3. Place the foil-wrapped pan in a large, deep baking pan, and pour boiling water into the larger pan until it reaches halfway up the outside of the cheesecake pan.

4. Bake for 60 minutes or until sides of cake appear firm and center jiggles slightly. (For a 9-inch pan, bake 50–55 minutes.) Turn off heat, open oven door, and let cheesecake cool in the oven for 30 minutes. Remove from water bath and finish cooling.

5. Refrigerate at least 6 hours before serving.

# Cheesecake Custard

*Serves Seven*

*If you are like me and love desserts for breakfast, this is your lucky day. This unique cheesecake-flavored custard delivers more protein than a large egg in a sweet-filled individual package. Because it's also low in sugar and carbs, it's also a blood sugar friendly way to start your day! For dessert enjoy it plain or top it with fresh berries, sliced bananas, or light whipped topping*

INGREDIENTS:

**1 8-ounce package light tub-style cream cheese**

**2 large eggs**

**2 large egg whites**

**⅔ cup Splenda Granulated sweetener**

**1 teaspoon vanilla extract**

**2½ cups 1% milk**

STEPS:

1. Preheat oven to 325°F.

2. In a medium bowl, beat together cream cheese, eggs, egg whites, sweetener, and vanilla extract. Set aside.

3. In a small saucepan, bring milk to a low simmer.

4. Whisk a small amount of hot milk into cream cheese mixture to temper the eggs. Whisk in remaining milk. Strain mixture into a large measuring cup with a pour spout.

5. Pour mixture into seven 6-ounce custard cups or ramekins. Place cups into a large baking dish and place in oven. Pour very hot water into baking dish until water reaches halfway up the sides of the custard cups.

6. Bake custard 45–55 minutes or until edges are set and centers slightly jiggle when shaken. Cool and refrigerate to set. Serve.

**PER SERVING**

| | |
|---|---|
| Calories 150 | Total Fat 8 grams |
| Carbohydrate 9 grams | Saturated Fat 5 grams |
| Sugars 7 grams | Protein 9 grams |
| Fiber 0 grams | Sodium 250 milligrams |

Diabetic exchange = ½ Low-Fat Milk, ½ Lean Meat, 1 Fat

WW point comparison = 4 points

*To reduce the fat, you may use 4 ounces each of nonfat and light cream cheese. I do not recommend using all nonfat cream cheese as it will affect both texture and taste.*

# Luscious Lemon Cheesecake

*Serves Twelve*

*The name says it all. This cheesecake is truly luscious. I sent it to work with my husband, and the cake was quickly gobbled up. No one ever suspected it wasn't a "regular" cheesecake. Mission accomplished!*

INGREDIENTS:

**1 9-inch baked Cheesecake Crumb Crust, page 117**

**1 cup low-fat cottage cheese**

**8 ounces tub-style light cream cheese**

**8 ounces nonfat cream cheese, room temperature**

**1 cup Splenda Granulated sweetener**

**2 tablespoons all-purpose flour**

**2 teaspoons cornstarch**

**2 teaspoons lemon juice**

**1 tablespoon lemon zest**

**1 8-ounce carton nonfat lemon yogurt (not light)**

**2 large eggs**

**2 large egg whites**

*Top this cake with sliced strawberries or raspberries, and then brush on 2 tablespoons of melted low-sugar jam for shine, or sift 2 teaspoons of powdered sugar over berries just before serving. So pretty!*

STEPS:

1. Preheat oven to 325°F. Wrap a 9-inch springform pan filled with crust tightly in heavy-duty foil (to make waterproof).

2. Place cottage cheese into a food processor or blender. Purée until completely smooth. Spoon into a large mixing bowl and add nonfat and light cream cheeses. Beat on medium speed with an electric mixer until creamy. Add the sweetener, flour, and cornstarch, and beat on low until smooth. Blend in the lemon juice, zest, and yogurt.

3. Add whole eggs and then egg whites, beating briefly after each addition to incorporate. Pour into the prepared pan and smooth top.

4. Place the foil-wrapped pan in a large deep baking pan and pour boiling water into larger pan until it reaches halfway up the outside of the cheesecake pan.

5. Bake for 60–65 minutes or until sides of cake appear firm and center jiggles slightly. Turn off the heat, open oven door and let cheesecake cool down in the oven for 30 minutes. Remove from water bath and finish cooling on rack.

6. Refrigerate at least 6 hours before serving.

**PER SERVING**

| | |
|---|---|
| Calories 160 | Total Fat 6 grams |
| Carbohydrate 15 grams | Saturated Fat 3.5 grams |
|    Sugars 5 grams | Protein 10 grams |
|    Fiber 0 grams | Sodium 340 milligrams |

Diabetic exchange = 1 Carbohydrate, 1½ Lean Meat
WW point comparison = 4 points

# Strawberry Swirl Cheesecake

*Serves Twelve*

*This is one gorgeous cheesecake. It's covered with a marbled strawberry topping that bakes right into the cheesecake. Because you can make it with either fresh or frozen strawberries, it can be enjoyed year-round.*

## INGREDIENTS:

1 9-inch baked **Cheesecake Crumb Crust**, page 117

1¼ cups fresh or frozen unsweetened strawberries

2 tablespoons low-sugar strawberry jam

2 tablespoons + 1¼ cups Splenda Granulated sweetener

2 teaspoons lemon juice

1 cup low-fat cottage cheese

8 ounces tub-style light cream cheese

8 ounces nonfat cream cheese, room temp

2 tablespoons all-purpose flour

2 tablespoons cornstarch

1 teaspoon vanilla extract

½ teaspoon almond extract

1 large egg

3 large egg whites

1¼ cups light sour cream

*Try substituting raspberries and low-sugar raspberry jam. Boysenberries are stunning, but force the purée through a sieve to remove the seeds before "swirling."*

### PER SERVING

| | |
|---|---|
| Calories 190 | Total Fat 8 grams |
| Carbohydrate 17 grams | Saturated Fat 5 grams |
| Sugars 8 grams | Protein 11 grams |
| Fiber 1 gram | Sodium 350 milligrams |

Diabetic exchange = 1 Carbohydrate, 1½ Lean Meat
WW point comparison = 4 points

## STEPS:

1. Preheat oven to 325°F. Wrap 9-inch springform pan filled with crust tightly in heavy-duty foil to waterproof.

2. Combine the strawberries, jam, 2 tablespoons sweetener, and lemon juice in a medium saucepan. Stir and cook until strawberries are soft and mushy. Use a fork to mash berries completely to form a thick strawberry purée (or you may want to use a food processor or blender). Set mixture aside to cool.

3. Purée cottage cheese in a food processor or blender until completely smooth. Spoon into a large mixing bowl and add both cream cheeses. Beat on medium speed with an electric mixer until creamy. Add 1¼ cup sweetener, flour, cornstarch, and extracts. Beat on low until smooth. Add whole egg and then egg whites, beating briefly after each addition. Stir in the sour cream with a large spoon. Pour into the prepared pan and smooth top.

4. Carefully place spoonfuls of the strawberry purée on top of the batter. Swirl a thin knife back and forth through the purée and batter to create a marbleized effect.

5. Place foil-wrapped pan in a large, deep baking pan and place on oven rack. Pour boiling water into larger pan until it reaches halfway up the outside of the cheesecake pan.

6. Bake for 70–75 minutes or until sides of cake appear firm and center jiggles slightly. Turn off heat, open oven door, and let cheesecake cool in the oven for 30 minutes. Remove from water bath and finish cooling. Refrigerate at least 6 hours before serving.

# Triple Chocolate Cheesecake

*Serves Twelve*

*Cheesecake and chocolate—how much better can it get? This creamy cake is for all you chocolate lovers. You start with a chocolate crumb crust, fill it with rich chocolate filling, and top the cheesecake with chocolate shavings (if that strikes your fancy). So, who said eating healthy isn't fun?*

INGREDIENTS:

1 9-inch Chocolate Cheesecake Crumb Crust, page 117

2 cups low-fat cottage cheese

8 ounces tub-style light cream cheese

8 ounces nonfat cream cheese, room temperature

½ cup semisweet chocolate chips, melted and cooled

1½ cups Splenda Granulated sweetener

4 tablespoons brown sugar

¼ cup Dutch-process cocoa powder (like Hershey's Special Dark)

2 tablespoons all-purpose flour

1 tablespoon cornstarch

1 teaspoon vanilla extract

½ teaspoon almond extract

1 large egg

3 large egg whites

½ cup light sour cream

1 1.5-ounce dark chocolate bar (optional)

---

PER SERVING

| | |
|---|---|
| Calories 220 | Total Fat 8 grams |
| Carbohydrate 24 grams | Saturated Fat 5 grams |
| Sugars 13 grams | Protein 13 grams |
| Fiber 1 gram | Sodium 380 milligrams |

Diabetic exchange = 1½ Carbohydrate, 2 Very Lean Meat
WW point comparison = 5 points

STEPS:

1. Preheat oven to 325°F. Wrap a 9-inch springform pan filled with crust tightly in heavy-duty foil to waterproof.

2. Place cottage cheese into a food processor or blender. Purée until completely smooth. Spoon into a large mixing bowl, and add nonfat and light cream cheeses. Beat on medium speed with an electric mixer until creamy. Add the cooled, melted chocolate and the next seven ingredients. Beat on low speed until smooth. Add whole egg and then egg whites, beating briefly after each addition to incorporate. Stir in the sour cream with a large spoon.

3. Pour mixture into the prepared pan and smooth top.

4. Place the foil-wrapped pan in a large, deep baking pan and pour boiling water into larger pan until it reaches halfway up the outside of the cheesecake pan.

5. Bake for 55–60 minutes or until sides of cake appear firm and center jiggles slightly. Turn off heat, open oven door, and let cheesecake cool in the oven for 30 minutes. Remove from water bath and finish cooling.

6. Refrigerate at least 6 hours before serving. Using a vegetable peeler, "peel" chocolate curls off the chocolate bar onto the cake.

# Black and White Cheesecake "Cupcakes"

*Serves Twelve*

*These cheesecake cupcakes are black-tie gorgeous. To serve, you can peel off the cupcake liners before placing on a serving plate, but I prefer to serve them in the liners, allowing the lucky recipient the joy of revealing the unexpected dark chocolate crust beneath the perfectly white layer of sour cream and cheesecake.*

INGREDIENTS:

CRUST

**4 full chocolate graham crackers (8 squares), crushed**

**2 tablespoons margarine, melted**

**2 tablespoons Splenda Granulated sweetener**

**1 tablespoon unsweetened cocoa powder**

FILLING

**8-ounce package light cream cheese, room temperature**

**4 ounces (½ package) fat-free cream cheese, room temperature**

**½ cup Splenda Granulated sweetener**

**1 large egg**

**1 large egg white**

**2 teaspoons lemon juice**

**1 teaspoon vanilla extract**

TOPPING

**½ cup sour cream**

**2 tablespoons Splenda Granulated sweetener**

**1 teaspoon vanilla extract**

---

**PER SERVING**

Calories 120                  Total Fat 7 grams
Carbohydrate 8 grams              Saturated Fat 4 grams
   Sugars 4 grams           Protein 5 grams
   Fiber 0 grams            Sodium 190 milligrams

Diabetic exchange = ½ Carbohydrate, 1 Fat
WW point comparison = 3 points

STEPS:

1. Preheat oven to 325°F. Place cupcake liners in 12-cup muffin tin and coat with nonstick cooking spray.

2. CRUST: In a small bowl, combine crushed graham crackers, margarine, sweetener, and cocoa powder; stir.

3. Spoon a heaping tablespoon of mixture into each cup and press down with your fingers or the back of a spoon to form a compact crust. Set aside.

4. FILLING: In a large bowl, using an electric mixer, beat cream cheeses and sweetener until combined. Add egg, egg white, lemon juice, and vanilla. Continue beating until all ingredients are incorporated. Spoon 2 tablespoons of cheesecake mixture into each cup and gently spread to even.

5. Bake 13–15 minutes until cheesecakes are just set. Remove from oven. Let cool slightly before topping.

6. TOPPING: In a small bowl, mix together sour cream, sweetener, and vanilla until combined. Spread 1 heaping teaspoon of mixture on top of each cheesecake.

7. Cool to room temperature and chill at least 2 hours before serving.

# Mocha Chip Cheesecake

*Serves Twelve*

*Coffee and chocolate—another great combination. This smooth cheesecake filling is lightly flavored with coffee and studded with miniature chocolate chips. It makes a great addition to any dinner party.*

INGREDIENTS:

**1 9-inch Chocolate Cheesecake Crumb Crust, page 117**

**1 cup low-fat cottage cheese**

**8 ounces tub-style light cream cheese**

**8 ounces nonfat cream cheese, room temperature**

**1½ cups Splenda Granulated sweetener**

**2 tablespoons all-purpose flour**

**1 tablespoon cornstarch**

**½ teaspoon vanilla extract**

**1 tablespoon + 1 teaspoon instant coffee powder**

**2 tablespoons hot water**

**2 large eggs**

**2 large egg whites**

**2 teaspoons all-purpose flour**

**⅔ cup mini chocolate chips**

STEPS:

1. Preheat oven to 325°F. Wrap a 9-inch springform pan filled with crust tightly in heavy-duty foil to waterproof.

2. Place cottage cheese into a food processor or blender. Purée until completely smooth. Spoon into a large mixing bowl and add nonfat and light cream cheeses. With an electric mixer, beat on medium until creamy. Add the sweetener, flour, cornstarch, and vanilla. Beat on low until smooth.

3. Dissolve coffee in the hot water and add to batter.

4. Add whole eggs and then egg whites, beating briefly after each addition to incorporate.

5. Coat the chocolate chips with 2 teaspoons of flour and stir in.

6. Pour into the prepared pan and smooth top. Place the foil-wrapped pan in a large, deep baking dish, and pour boiling water into larger pan until it reaches halfway up the outside of the cheesecake pan.

7. Bake for 60 minutes or until sides of cake appear firm and center jiggles slightly. Turn off heat, open oven door, and let cheesecake cool in oven for 30 minutes. Remove from water bath and finish cooling.

8. Refrigerate at least 6 hours before serving.

**PER SERVING**

| | |
|---|---|
| Calories 220 | Total Fat 10 grams |
| Carbohydrate 22 grams | Saturated Fat 6 grams |
| Sugars 12 grams | Protein 11 grams |
| Fiber 1 gram | Sodium 350 milligrams |

Diabetic exchange = 1½ Carbohydrate, 1½ Medium-Fat Meat

WW point comparison = 5 points

# Pumpkin Streusel Cheesecake

*Serves Twelve*

*As featured on the Today Show, this star of a cheesecake is one of my favorite desserts for the holidays. It looks festive and tastes fabulous. In the past, I've made it many times using sugar, but I'm happy to say that this sugar-free version is just as good as the original.*

INGREDIENTS:

CRUST

18 gingersnap cookies, ground into crumbs
   (may substitute graham-cracker crumbs)
¼ cup Splenda Granulated sweetener
1 tablespoon light margarine or butter,
   melted

FILLING

1 cup low-fat cottage cheese
8 ounces tub-style light cream cheese
8 ounces nonfat cream cheese,
   room temperature
1¼ cups Splenda Granulated sweetener
1 15-ounce can solid pack pumpkin
1 tablespoon all-purpose flour
2 tablespoons cornstarch
1 teaspoon cinnamon
½ teaspoon ground ginger
½ teaspoon allspice
1 teaspoon vanilla extract
2 large eggs
4 large egg whites
½ cup light sour cream

STREUSEL

¼ cup all-purpose flour
1 tablespoon brown sugar
1 tablespoon light butter, cold

Continues on next page . . .

---

**PER SERVING**

Calories 200                    Total Fat 7 grams
Carbohydrate 21 grams            Saturated Fat 4 grams
   Sugars 9 grams               Protein 11 grams
   Fiber 2 grams                Sodium 370 milligrams

Diabetic exchange = 1½ Carbohydrate, 1½ Medium-Fat
   Meat
WW point comparison = 4 points

STEPS:

1. Preheat oven to 325°F. Spray a 9-inch springform pan with nonstick cooking spray.

2. CRUST: In a small bowl, combine the cookie crumbs with the sweetener. Add the butter and stir to mix. Reserve ⅓ cup of the crumbs and press rest of crumbs onto the bottom of prepared pan.

3. Bake for 5 minutes. Set aside.

4. FILLING: Place cottage cheese into a food processor or blender. Purée until completely smooth. Spoon into a large mixing bowl and add nonfat and light cream cheeses. With an electric mixer, beat on medium until creamy.

5. Add the sweetener, pumpkin, flour, cornstarch, spices, and vanilla. Beat on low speed until smooth. Add whole eggs and then egg whites, beating briefly after each addition to incorporate. Stir in the sour cream with a large spoon.

6. Pour into the prepared crust and smooth top.

7. Bake for 75 minutes or until the sides are firm and the center jiggles slightly.

8. STREUSEL: Add flour and brown sugar to the reserved cookie crumbs. Cut in butter until a loose crumb forms. After baking cheesecake, open oven and sprinkle crumbs over entire cake (covering any cracks). Place back in oven for an additional 15 minutes. Turn off heat, open door, and let cheesecake cool in oven for 30 minutes. Remove from oven and place on rack to cool.

9. Refrigerate at least 6 hours before serving. Best if made a day or two in advance.

# Blueberry Cheesecake Parfaits

*Serves Six*

*This recipe has become one of my all-time favorite desserts. It's really fun, the presentation is original, and everyone loves it. Besides looking incredible, it's sweet, rich, and creamy. You'll love it, too, because it's simple to prepare, and yet looks and tastes very impressive. These are also fabulous for entertaining because they are individually portioned and can be made ahead of time. Voilà!*

INGREDIENTS:

½ **cup graham-cracker crumbs**

2 **tablespoons Splenda Granulated sweetener**

1½ **tablespoons light butter**

4 **ounces tub-style light cream cheese**

4 **ounces nonfat cream cheese, room temperature**

½ **cup light sour cream**

¼ **cup Splenda Granulated sweetener**

1 **cup light whipped topping, thawed**

1½ **cups fresh blueberries**★

★Feel free to substitute your favorite berries or chopped fresh fruit!

STEPS:

1. Select 6 tall stemmed glasses. (An 8-ounce wineglass or champagne glass is ideal.)

2. In a small bowl, mix graham-cracker crumbs, 2 tablespoons sweetener, and butter. Set aside.

3. In a medium mixing bowl, beat cream cheeses with an electric mixer until creamy. Add sour cream and ¼ cup sweetener and stir until smooth. Fold in light whipped topping with a spoon or spatula.

4. In the bottom of each glass, place 1 tablespoon graham cracker mix. Press down with spoon. Place about 3 tablespoons of cream cheese mix on top of each. (You will use only ½ of the cheese mixture for the 6 glasses.) Divide the berries among the glasses, placing them on top of the cream cheese layer. Add one more layer of cream cheese. Finish the parfait by topping each with 1 tablespoon of crumbs.

5. Enjoy immediately or place in the refrigerator until ready to be served.

**PER SERVING**

| | |
|---|---|
| Calories 185 | Total Fat 8 grams |
| Carbohydrate 20 grams | Saturated Fat 6 grams |
| Sugars 12 grams | Protein 7 grams |
| Fiber 1 gram | Sodium 280 milligrams |

Diabetic exchange = 1 Carbohydrate, 1 Low-Fat Meat, 1 Fat
WW point comparison = 4 points

# Key Lime Cheesecake

*Serves Twelve*

*If you like key lime pie, this is the cheesecake for you. It has a lighter texture than most cheesecakes, and, of course, has the wonderful tartness of key limes. Key lime juice can be found next to the bottled lemon juice in most markets.*

INGREDIENTS:

**1 9-inch Cheesecake Crumb Crust, page 117**

**1 envelope unflavored gelatin (2½ teaspoons)**

**¾ cup key lime juice**

**1 cup Splenda Granulated sweetener**

**2 large eggs, lightly beaten**

**8 ounces tub-style light cream cheese**

**8 ounces nonfat cream cheese, room temperature**

**4 large pasteurized egg whites (or 2 regular egg whites★)**

**¾ cup Splenda Granulated sweetener**

**1½ cups light whipped topping**

★See page 22 for information regarding the safety of raw eggs.

_____

**PER SERVING**

| | |
|---|---|
| Calories 160 | Total Fat 7.5 grams |
| Carbohydrate 16 grams | Saturated Fat 4 grams |
|   Sugars 6 grams | Protein 7 grams |
|   Fiber 0 grams | Sodium 270 milligrams |

Diabetic exchange = 1 Carbohydrate, 1 Lean Meat, 1 Fat
WW point comparison = 4 points

STEPS:

1. In a medium saucepan, dissolve the gelatin in the key lime juice for 3 minutes. Add 1 cup of sweetener and the 2 beaten eggs.

2. Place on stove and turn heat to medium while stirring, and cook for 10 minutes or until mixture thickens. Remove from heat. Cool slightly.

3. Place the cream cheese in a large bowl, and beat on medium speed with an electric mixer until creamy. Slowly add the lime mixture and beat on low until smooth. Refrigerate mixture until thoroughly cooled, stirring every 10 minutes.

4. In a separate bowl, beat the egg whites until foamy or until soft peaks begin to form; this can take 5 minutes or more with pasteurized egg whites. Slowly add the ¾ cup sweetener until incorporated.

5. Fold egg white mixture into the chilled lime-cheese mix. Pour onto prepared crust.

6. Refrigerate until set, about 2 hours.

7. Spread whipped topping over cake.

*The original recipe for this yummy and sweet yet tart cheesecake had 40 grams of sugar per piece.*

# Chocolate Peppermint Cheesecake

*Serves Ten (I usually cut 12 pieces, but splurge—it's Christmas!)*

*Here it is—your Christmas cheesecake. It's wonderful. Start with a chocolate crumb crust that is filled with a peppermint-flecked cream cheese mixture, and finish with crushed peppermint candies and chocolate on the top. No, you're not dreaming. This cheesecake is still low in sugar, fat, and calories. And, best of all—it's a cinch to make, leaving you free for all your other holiday chores.*

INGREDIENTS:

1 Chocolate Cheesecake Crumb Crust, page 117

1 envelope unflavored gelatin

¼ cup cold water

8 ounces tub-style light cream cheese

8 ounces nonfat cream cheese, room temperature

½ cup Splenda Granulated sweetener

3 tablespoons 1% milk

12 sugar-free peppermint hard candies, finely crushed

½ teaspoon peppermint extract

1½ cups light whipped topping, thawed

6 sugar-free peppermint hard candies, crushed

1 1.5-ounce milk chocolate bar or semisweet chocolate bar

STEPS:

1. In a small saucepan, sprinkle the gelatin over water; let stand for 3 minutes. Place over low heat, stirring, until gelatin dissolves. Remove from heat.

2. In a large mixing bowl, beat the cream cheeses and sweetener with an electric mixer until creamy. Add the gelatin mixture and the milk. Beat on low speed until smooth.

3. Stir in the 12 crushed peppermints and the extract. Chill until the mixture mounds slightly when dropped from a spoon.

4. Fold in the whipped topping. Pour into the prepared crust and smooth top.

5. Refrigerate at least 3 hours.

6. Before serving, sprinkle top of the cake with remaining crushed peppermint candies. As a final decorative touch, use a vegetable peeler to shave chocolate curls directly onto the top of the cake—and wait for the oohs and aahs.

*I found my sugar-free hard peppermints in the candy aisle of my local grocery.*

PER SERVING

| | |
|---|---|
| Calories 190 | Total Fat 8 grams |
| Carbohydrate 22 grams | Saturated Fat 5 grams |
| Sugars 14 grams | Protein 8 grams |
| Fiber 0 grams | Sodium 320 milligrams |

Diabetic exchange = 1½ Carbohydrate, 1 Lean Meat, 1 Fat

WW point comparison = 4 points

# 10-Minute No-Bake Strawberry Cheese Pie

*Serves Eight*

*This is a snap to make and very pretty to serve. If you want to make it a day ahead, simply cover the cheese-filled pie and place it in the refrigerator. Within 1 to 2 hours of serving time, cover with the fresh berries and glaze.*

INGREDIENTS:

1 low-fat store-bought graham-cracker crumb crust

½ cup low-fat cottage cheese

4 ounces light cream cheese

¼ cup Splenda Granulated sweetener

2 tablespoons low-sugar strawberry jam, melted

½ cup light sour cream

1½ cups strawberry slices (8 ounces fresh berries)

2 tablespoons low-sugar strawberry jam

STEPS:

1. Place the cottage cheese in a food processor or blender and purée until entirely smooth.

2. Pour into a medium bowl and beat in cream cheese, sweetener, and jam with an electric mixer. Stir in sour cream and spoon mixture into crust.

3. Arrange strawberry slices in a decorative manner to cover top of pie.

4. Melt 2 tablespoons of jam (microwave 20–30 seconds on high) and strain by pouring it through a mesh strainer.

5. Brush strained jam over berries.

6. Refrigerate for 1–2 hours before serving.

*This is a great grab-and-go pie. The first time I made it, I took it to my mother-in-law's for dinner. Since then, she has made it many times for friends who watch their diets. Don't forget to keep it cool during your travels.*

**PER SERVING**

Calories 180

Carbohydrate 22 grams

　Sugars 12 grams

　Fiber 2 grams

Total Fat 7 grams

　Saturated Fat 3 grams

Protein 7 grams

Sodium 260 milligrams

Diabetic exchange = ½ Carbohydrate, ½ Fruit, ½ Low-Fat Milk, 1 Fat

WW point comparison = 4 points

# Puddings and Specialty Desserts

Some desserts are extra-special. They are the ones you rarely, if ever, make and yet relish every time you eat them. They are often the types of desserts that don't fit into the more common categories of cakes, pies, and cookies. I've included those special recipes in this chapter. Decadent items like cream puffs, mousses, and soufflés. Traditional treats like shortcakes and strudels, and comforting favorites like a bowl of homemade warm pudding. And adding to the mix, I've included three new recipes: Quick 'n' Healthy Creamy Rice Pudding, Strawberry Buttermilk Panna Cotta, and Creamy Frozen Fruit Bars. Many of these desserts hold great memories for me—and perhaps for you, too. If you have eliminated these incredible sweets from your diet because of health concerns, you're in luck, because you can truly enjoy these favorites any time. Every dessert in this chapter has fewer than 200 calories per serving (The "Marvel-ous" Lemon Mousse has only 100!) and is low in fat and sugar. But what is really incredible is that they look and taste tremendous. Now that is special!

# Vanilla Pudding

*Serves Five*

*When it comes to pudding at my house, we have the vanilla camp versus the chocolate camp. I definitely belong to the first camp, especially when it comes to smooth, sweet, creamy puddings like this one. This rich vanilla pudding stands on its own as a prized homestyle dessert, but it can also be used in your favorite parfait recipes, or as filling for a vanilla cream pie.*

## INGREDIENTS:

3 tablespoons cornstarch

⅔ cup Splenda Granulated sweetener

½ cup nonfat half-and-half

1 large egg + 1 egg yolk, slightly beaten

1¾ cups 1% milk

1½ teaspoons vanilla extract

## STEPS:

1. In a medium saucepan, combine the cornstarch, sweetener, half-and-half, and beaten egg. Whisk until smooth. Whisk in 1% milk.

2. Cook and stir over medium heat until the pudding is thick and bubbly. Cook for 1 minute more. Remove from heat. Stir in the vanilla.

3. Pour into medium bowl or divide among 5 dessert dishes. Cover with plastic wrap. Cool and refrigerate until served.

VANILLA PIE FILLING: Add 1 additional tablespoon of cornstarch to recipe to fill a 9-inch pie.

*Nonfat half-and-half adds richness without fat to this pudding; you may substitute evaporated skim milk or additional 1% milk for nonfat half-and-half if preferred.*

## PER SERVING

| | |
|---|---|
| Calories 110 | Total Fat 3 grams |
| Carbohydrate 15 grams | Saturated Fat 1 gram |
| Sugars 4 grams | Protein 4 grams |
| Fiber 0 grams | Sodium 60 milligrams |

Diabetic exchange = ½ Low-Fat Milk, ½ Carbohydrate

WW point comparison = 2 points

# Double Chocolate Pudding

*Serves Six*

*This pudding is for the chocolate lovers in your household. A rich and creamy chocolate version, this pudding puts packaged sugar-free counterparts to shame. A special occasion is not a requirement, but this pudding will make any day seem out of the ordinary.*

INGREDIENTS:

3 tablespoons cornstarch

¾ cup Splenda Granulated sweetener

2 tablespoons Dutch-process cocoa powder (like Hershey's Special Dark)

½ cup nonfat half-and-half

1 large egg, slightly beaten

1¾ cups 1% milk

⅓ cup chocolate chips

1½ teaspoons vanilla extract

STEPS:

1. In a medium saucepan, combine the cornstarch, sweetener, cocoa powder, half-and-half, and beaten egg. Whisk until smooth. Whisk in 1% milk.

2. Cook and stir over medium heat until the pudding is thick and bubbly. Cook for 1 minute more. Remove from heat.

3. Stir in the chocolate chips, whisking until melted. Stir in vanilla.

4. Pour into a medium bowl or divide among 6 dessert dishes. Cover with plastic wrap. Cool and refrigerate until served.

*Double the treat: In a tall glass, alternate layers of chocolate and vanilla pudding for a "zebra" parfait.*

PER SERVING

| | |
|---|---|
| Calories 130 | Total Fat 4.5 grams |
| Carbohydrate 18 grams | Saturated Fat 2.5 grams |
| Sugars 8 grams | Protein 4 grams |
| Fiber 0 grams | Sodium 65 milligrams |

Diabetic exchange = ½ Low-Fat Milk, ½ Carbohydrate, ½ Fat

WW point comparison = 3 points

# Quick 'n' Healthy Creamy Rice Pudding

*Serves Six*

*Good health and great taste are joined hand in hand in this irresistible stove-top rice pudding. Made with healthy brown rice, almond "milk," and nonfat half-and-half, it's creamy and incredibly rich tasting with a fraction of the fat, carbs, and calories of traditional rice puddings. A touch of cinnamon and orange are the perfect flavor complements. We found ourselves eating spoonful after spoonful (in the name of "tasting," of course), as did my husband, who found it so delicious he had to be assured more than once that it was truly healthy. (A healthy note: unsweetened almond milk has only forty calories and 2 grams of carbohydrate per cup, compared with 150 calories and 6 grams of carbohydrate per cup of milk.)*

## INGREDIENTS:

¾ cup cold water

½ cup quick-cooking brown rice (like Uncle Ben's)

2¼ cups unsweetened almond milk

½ cup Splenda Granulated sweetener

¾ teaspoon cinnamon

⅛ teaspoon salt

¾ cup nonfat half-and-half

2 teaspoons cornstarch

1 teaspoon vanilla extract

¾ teaspoon orange zest

*Almond milk is a creamy, mild-tasting beverage made from pressed almonds and filtered water. It's a great lower-calorie, lactose-free alternative to milk and other nondairy beverages such as soy milk. You will find it in the supermarket next to the nonrefrigerated soy milks.*

## STEPS:

1. In a medium saucepan, bring water to a boil, and stir in rice. Reduce to simmer, cover, and cook for 10 minutes or until water is absorbed.

2. Stir in milk, sweetener, cinnamon, and salt. Cook, uncovered, over medium heat for 25 minutes, stirring occasionally.

3. Stir cornstarch into half-and-half and add to rice. Stir in vanilla and orange zest. Stir and cook until bubbling. Cook on low for 1 minute longer and remove from heat. (Pudding will continue to thicken upon cooling.) Pour into a serving bowl or dessert dishes and let cool. Serve or cover and refrigerate until served.

OLD-FASHIONED VARIATION: Use white rice for quick-cooking brown rice and 1% milk for almond milk (adds 25 calories and 6 grams of carbohydrate per serving).

## PER SERVING (½ CUP)

| | |
|---|---|
| Calories 105 | Total Fat 2 grams |
| Carbohydrate 19 grams | Saturated Fat 0 grams |
| Sugars 0 grams | Protein 3 grams |
| Fiber 1 gram | Sodium 80 milligrams |

Diabetic exchange = 1 Carbohydrate

WW point comparison = 1 point

# Pumpkin Custard Cups

*Serves Seven*

*The best part of pumpkin pie is the rich pumpkin filling, of course. Here is a recipe that gives you that delicious filling without the added calories and work of a crust. Another bonus—adding an extra egg yolk and baking the filled cups in a water bath are two steps that produce an even creamier custard texture than you achieve with a pie.*

INGREDIENTS:

**1 recipe Pumpkin Pie filling, page 85**
**1 egg yolk**

STEPS:

1. Preheat oven to 350°F. Spray seven 6-ounce custard or soufflé cups with nonstick cooking spray.

2. Prepare the pie filling according to the directions (eliminating the crust and the beaten egg white wash) using 1 additional egg yolk (you can simply substitute 1 additional large whole egg for 1 of the egg whites).

3. Pour the filling into the cups, and place cups in a large, deep baking pan. Pour boiling water into the baking pan until it reaches halfway up the sides of the cups.

4. Bake for 40 minutes or until a knife inserted near the centers of the custards comes out clean.

*Individual servings not only make desserts easy to serve, but they're also great for portion control.*

**PER SERVING**

Calories 120
Carbohydrate 17 grams
   Sugars 10 grams
   Fiber 2 grams

Total Fat 1.5 grams
   Saturated Fat 0.5 gram
Protein 8 grams
Sodium 100 milligrams

Diabetic exchange = ½ Carbohydrate, ½ Low-Fat Milk, ½ Vegetable
WW point comparison = 2 points

# Strawberry Buttermilk Panna Cotta

*Serves Eight*

*Panna cotta, when translated, means "cooked cream" in Italian. It is a traditional, very popular, and easy-to-make dessert found all over Italy. This particular recipe was created by an innovative pastry chef with whom I once worked. Her modern take on tradition replaces high-fat cream with tangy buttermilk for an exciting new taste twist. I find this recipe best when made a day ahead of time and then eaten after letting the panna cotta warm slightly (about five minutes) after removing it from the refrigerator.*

INGREDIENTS:

3 tablespoons cold water

1 packet unflavored gelatin

1 cup light sour cream

2½ cups buttermilk

1½ teaspoons vanilla extract

½ cup Splenda Granulated sweetener

½ cup light or sugar-free strawberry jam

STEPS:

1. Lightly coat eight 6-ounce ramekins with nonstick cooking spray.

2. Sprinkle gelatin over water and let set for 3 minutes to soften.

3. In a medium saucepan over low heat, mix sour cream, buttermilk, vanilla extract, and sweetener. Stirring constantly, bring mixture to a gentle simmer. Add gelatin and stir until dissolved. Immediately remove from heat. (Be careful not to boil mixture.)

4. Stir in jam until thoroughly incorporated. Pour ½ cup of the buttermilk mixture into each ramekin. Chill in the refrigerator for at least 4 hours or until firmly set.

5. Serve turned out onto a plate or in ramekins.

*To make unmolding the panna cotta easy, dip each ramekin in a small bowl of hot water for a few seconds before turning out onto a plate.*

PER SERVING

| | |
|---|---|
| Calories 90 | Total Fat 3.5 grams |
| Carbohydrate 8 grams | Saturated Fat 2.5 grams |
| Sugars 6 grams | Sodium 120 milligrams |
| Fiber 0 grams | Protein 6 grams |

Diabetic exchange = ½ Low-Fat Milk, ½ Fat
WW point comparison = 2 points

# Creamy Frozen Fruit Bars

*Serves Five*

*Enjoy the summer pleasure of icy Popsicles. Here you'll find two versions—the creamy one will remind you more of an ice cream bar, while the all-juice version provides the familiar and refreshingly juicy sweetness of a true Popsicle.*

INGREDIENTS:

**2 cups mixed berries, fresh or frozen, completely thawed**

**½ cup light cranberry juice**

**½ cup buttermilk**

**½ cup Splenda Granulated sweetener**

*For a nondairy all-juice pop, eliminate the buttermilk and use 1 cup light cranberry juice.*

STEPS:

1. Place all ingredients into a blender or food processor and blend until smooth.

2. Strain berry mixture by pouring it through a fine mesh strainer to remove the seeds, using a spoon to push juice through mesh as needed. Pour the strained mixture into an ice-pop mold or 5-ounce disposable paper cups.

3. Add sticks to molds or tightly place a piece of foil over each cup. Push pop sticks through the foil into the middle of each pop and place in freezer.

4. To remove pops, rub a kitchen towel with hot water over the molds. Serve immediately.

---

**PER SERVING (1 POP)**

Calories 60

Carbohydrate 11 grams

  Sugars 8 grams

  Fiber 2 grams

Total Fat .5 grams

  Saturated Fat 0 grams

Protein 2 grams

Sodium 40 milligrams

Diabetic exchange = 1 Fruit

WW point comparison = 1 point

# "Marvel-ous" Lemon Mousse

### Serves Six

*I call this "marvel-ous" because this recipe is a marvel of good nutrition. It is filled with things that are good for you, like protein, vitamin C, and calcium—all packed into 100 slim calories. Cool, creamy, and sweet with a nice tart touch of lemon, "Marvel-ous" Lemon Mousse is unbelievably good for you but so tasty you'll find it hard to believe it.*

INGREDIENTS:

**1 envelope unflavored gelatin**

**⅔ cup lemon juice**

**¾ cup Splenda Granulated sweetener**

**Finely grated zest of 1 lemon**

**2 drops yellow food coloring (optional)**

**½ cup cottage cheese**

**8 ounces nonfat plain yogurt**

**1 egg white (pasteurized or powdered, if preferred)**

**1 tablespoon sugar**

**¾ cup light whipped topping**

STEPS:

1. Place the gelatin in a small saucepan. Add ⅓ cup of the lemon juice and let stand for 3 minutes. Place on low heat and add remaining ⅓ cup of lemon juice, sweetener, zest and food coloring if desired. Heat for 3–4 minutes until gelatin is completely dissolved. Transfer mixture to a bowl.

2. Set aside and allow to cool slightly. Stir occasionally so mixture does not gel. Purée cottage cheese and yogurt until completely smooth (like sour cream).

3. Whisk purée into the lemon-gelatin mixture. Place mixture in the refrigerator to cool, whisking occasionally to prevent lumps. Beat the egg white to soft peaks. Add 1 tablespoon of sugar and beat until stiff, but not dry. Fold into the cooled lemon mixture. Fold in light whipped topping and pour into desired serving dish or serving cups.

*Although light and creamy, this mousse is firm enough to be spooned into bite-sized tart shells, like those made from filo dough found in your grocer's freezer case, or a pie shell to make a Lemon Mousse Pie. Any way you serve it, it is beautiful when garnished with fresh berries and mint leaves.*

**PER SERVING**

| | |
|---|---|
| Calories 100 | Total Fat 1.5 grams |
| Carbohydrate 13 grams | Saturated Fat 1 gram |
| Sugars 8 grams | Protein 9 grams |
| Fiber 0 grams | Sodium 55 milligrams |

Diabetic exchange = 1 Very Low-Fat Milk
WW point comparison = 2 points

# Tiramisu in a Glass

*Serves Six*

*Tiramisu is a beloved Italian dessert that contains a rich, smooth, Italian cream cheese called mascarpone that is loaded with fat. Combine this with the cream, egg yolks, and sugar traditionally used to make tiramisu, and you have one heavy dessert. In this recipe, I've kept some of the mascarpone for its unique flavor, but lightened the additional ingredients. I have also chosen a unique and contemporary way to serve it by assembling individual portions in martini glasses. You may also layer ingredients in a large serving dish as described below.*

INGREDIENTS:

**4 ounces mascarpone cheese★**

**4 ounces nonfat cream cheese**

**¼ cup low-fat ricotta cheese**

**2 tablespoons light sour cream**

**½ cup Splenda Granulated sweetener**

**¾ cup light whipped topping**

**¾ cup water**

**1 tablespoon instant coffee**

**3 tablespoons Splenda Granulated sweetener**

**1 tablespoon brandy (optional)**

**1 3-ounce package ladyfingers
(you need 12 split fingers)**

**1 teaspoon Dutch-process cocoa powder
(like Hershey's Special Dark)**

**½ ounce semisweet chocolate,
shaved (optional)**

★You can substitute 4 ounces tub-style light cream cheese and 2 tablespoons light sour cream.

**PER SERVING**

Calories 160

Carbohydrate 9 grams

   Sugars 3 grams

   Fiber 0 grams

Total Fat 11 grams

   Saturated Fat 4.5 grams

Protein 5 grams

Sodium 135 milligrams

Diabetic exchange = ½ Carbohydrate, 1 Very Lean Meat, 2 Fat

WW point comparison = 4 points

STEPS:

1. Gather 6 standard martini glasses (about 6 ounces each) or a 1-quart serving dish. In a medium mixing bowl, beat the mascarpone and the next 4 ingredients with an electric mixer until creamy and smooth. Fold in the light whipped topping. Set aside.

2. Place the water in a small microwaveable bowl or saucepan. Add the instant coffee and sweetener—and brandy, if desired—and heat for 2 minutes.

3. To ASSEMBLE INDIVIDUAL TIRAMISUS: For each tiramisu, lightly dip the outside of 4 ladyfinger pieces (2 whole ladyfingers, each split in half), in coffee mixture and place standing up against the sides of the martini glass. Brush the inside of the ladyfingers with more coffee. Place ½ cup of cheese mixture in the center of the ladyfingers. Sift small amount (⅛ teaspoon) of the cocoa powder over the cheese mixture. Top with a touch of shaved chocolate, if desired. Wrap glass with plastic wrap and refrigerate for 6 hours before serving.

*I have featured this recipe many times while teaching cooking classes. It has concluded classes on pasta, healthy low-carb cooking, and sugar-free baking, and every time, it's a hit. Students have told me they made it for friends, and their friends have gone on to make it for their friends, and that's the sincerest compliment of all.*

4. To ASSEMBLE IN A SINGLE DISH: Place half of the ladyfingers on the bottom of the dish. Brush ladyfingers with half of the coffee mixture. Top with half of the cheese mixture and smooth.

5. Repeat. Sift the cocoa powder over the top of the tiramisu. Top with the shaved chocolate, if desired. Refrigerate for 6 hours before serving.

# Chocolate Mousse Cake

## Serves Eight

*My parents happened to be in town the day I made this cake. After dinner, I served it to my father, a lover of all things rich, sweet, and fattening. When I asked him what he thought, he answered with one word—"decadent." Unlike most cakes, this incredible dessert has the light, creamy, rich texture of mousse. It sits on a chocolate crumb crust, but unlike mousse, can be sliced like a cake. Thus, I call it a mousse "cake." My dad prefers to call it delicious.*

INGREDIENTS:

CRUST

¾ cup chocolate graham-cracker crumbs

1 tablespoon Splenda Granulated sweetener

1 teaspoon unsweetened Dutch-process cocoa powder (like Hershey's Special Dark)

2 tablespoons margarine

FILLING

1 envelope unsweetened gelatin (2½ teaspoons)

¼ cup water

1 cup 1% milk

1 large egg, lightly beaten

⅓ cup unsweetened Dutch-process cocoa powder

⅔ cup Splenda Granulated sweetener

⅓ cup semisweet chocolate chips

1 teaspoon vanilla extract

¼ teaspoon orange extract or 1 tablespoon orange liqueur

2 large egg whites (or 3 pasteurized, if preferred)

1 tablespoon sugar

1 cup light whipped topping, thawed

½ ounce chocolate shavings (optional)

**PER SERVING**

| | |
|---|---|
| Calories 175 | Total Fat 7.5 grams |
| Carbohydrate 24 grams | Saturated Fat 3.5 grams |
| Sugars 14 grams | Protein 5 grams |
| Fiber 1.5 grams | Sodium 130 milligrams |

Diabetic exchange = 1 Carbohydrate, 1 Lean Meat, 1 Fat
WW point comparison = 4 points

STEPS:

1. Preheat oven to 350°F. Spray a 9-inch springform pan with nonstick cooking spray.

2. CRUST: In a small bowl, combine the graham-cracker crumbs, sweetener, and cocoa powder. Add the margarine and stir to mix.

3. Press crumbs onto bottom and 1½ inches up the sides of the prepared pan (pressing with plastic wrap will help with the sides). Bake for 8 minutes. Cool.

4. FILLING: In a medium saucepan, sprinkle gelatin over ¼ cup of water. Let stand 3 minutes.

5. Whisk in milk, beaten egg, cocoa powder, and sweetener. Place on stove and turn heat to medium. Cook, stirring until thickened and smooth. Add chocolate chips and stir until melted. Stir in vanilla and orange extract. Remove from heat. Pour into a large bowl and let cool.

6. Refrigerate for 30 minutes, stirring occasionally until mixture is cold and begins to mound when dropped from a spoon.

7. Beat egg whites until frothy. Add sugar and continue to beat until stiff, but not dry. Fold egg whites into chocolate mixture. Fold in light whipped topping. Pour mousse into crust and smooth. Refrigerate for at least 2 hours. Garnish with a touch of chocolate shavings, if desired.

# Cold Strawberry Soufflé

*Serves Eight*

*This is one of the first recipes I developed with Splenda. I made it and took it to a dinner party, and everyone loved it. My friends commented on how light and creamy it was. They also noted the fresh strawberry flavor. What they didn't comment on was the fact that the sugar had been replaced. This told me what I really wanted to know—that Splenda could sweeten my favorite desserts with the same wonderful taste of sugar.*

## INGREDIENTS:

**2 pints fresh strawberries (approximately 2 pounds)**

**2 envelopes unflavored gelatin (2½ teaspoons each)**

**½ cup Splenda Granulated sweetener**

**1 tablespoon lemon juice**

**6 large egg whites or 9 pasteurized egg whites + ½ teaspoon cream of tartar**

**1 8-ounce container light whipped topping, thawed**

*Using regular egg whites achieves the greatest egg white volume with the fewest eggs. Be sure eggs are fresh and clean, and have no cracks. For extra safety, when making this dessert for kids, the elderly, or those with compromised immune systems, use egg white powder or pasteurized egg whites.*

## STEPS:

1. Set aside a 2-quart soufflé dish or bowl.

2. Clean, stem, and halve berries. You should have about 5 cups. Reserve four berries for garnish.

3. Purée the remaining berries in a food processor or blender. Place 1 cup of purée in a medium saucepan. Add gelatin and ¼ cup sweetener. Heat until gelatin dissolves. Add the rest of the purée and the lemon juice. Remove from heat and chill for 20 minutes.

4. While purée is chilling, beat egg whites until foamy. Add remaining sweetener and continue to beat until stiff but not dry. Fold ¼ of the egg whites into the cooled purée. Gently fold in the remaining egg whites. Fold in the light whipped topping.

5. Spoon into the soufflé dish and chill in the refrigerator for at least 4 hours before serving.

6. Just before serving, garnish the top of the soufflé with the reserved berries.

### PER SERVING

Calories 120

Carbohydrate 16 grams

Sugars 10 grams

Fiber 1 gram

Total Fat 4 grams

Saturated Fat 3.5 grams

Protein 5 grams

Sodium 45 milligrams

Diabetic exchange = 1 Medium-Fat Meat, ½ Fruit

WW point comparison = 2 points

# Amazing Cream Puffs

*Serves Eight*

*Cream puffs are extraordinary treats and although not difficult to make, they require three steps: the puff, the cream filling, and the chocolate fudge topping. You can make the puffs a day ahead or earlier and freeze them. The filling keeps for one day, and the Chocolate Fudge Sauce keeps for a week (unless you eat it sooner). You may prepare the puffs in separate steps if you prefer. However, they are best eaten within a day, which is rarely a problem.*

INGREDIENTS:

PUFFS

½ cup water

3 tablespoons butter

¼ teaspoon salt

½ cup all-purpose flour

1 large egg

3 large egg whites

FILLING

1 recipe Vanilla Pudding (omitting ½ cup nonfat half-and-half) (page 133)

½ cup light whipped topping

TOPPING

⅓ cup Chocolate Fudge Sauce (page 156)

STEPS:

1. Preheat oven to 300°F. Spray a baking sheet with nonstick cooking spray.

2. PUFFS: In a medium saucepan, bring the water, butter, and salt to a boil. Add flour, all at once, and stir until the mixture is smooth and pulls away from the sides to form a ball. Remove from heat. Let cool 3 minutes. Add egg and then egg whites, beating vigorously after each addition until mixture is smooth and shiny again. Using a tablespoon, spoon dough onto prepared baking pan, making 8 mounds. Place pan in lower third of oven and turn heat up to 450°F. Bake 15 minutes, until dough is well puffed and brown. Reduce temperature to 300°F and bake 15 more minutes. Cut a small slit on the side of each puff to allow steam to escape; turn off heat and allow puffs to dry for 5 minutes in the oven. Remove and place on rack to cool. Once cool, puffs can be kept 1 day in an airtight container or wrapped well and frozen.

*Continues on next page . . .*

---

**PER SERVING**

| | |
|---|---|
| Calories 170 | Total Fat 8 grams |
| Carbohydrate 18 grams | Saturated Fat 4 grams |
| Sugars 3 grams | Protein 6 grams |
| Fiber 0 grams | Sodium 70 milligrams |

Diabetic exchange = 1 Carbohydrate, 1 Lean Meat, 1 Fat

WW point comparison = 4 points

3. To PREPARE FILLING: Prepare pudding according to directions. Chill. When cold, fold in whipped topping ¼ cup at a time. Fold in rest of topping. The filling can be kept covered and refrigerated for 1 day.

4. TOPPING: Prepare chocolate fudge sauce according to directions. If prepared in advance, heat lightly to a pourable consistency before using.

5. To ASSEMBLE CREAM PUFFS: Cut top off each puff. Remove any wet or loose dough to create a clean cavity. Fill with ¼ cup cream filling and replace top. Drizzle 2 teaspoons of Chocolate Fudge Sauce over the top of each cream puff.

*Starting the puffs in a moderate temperature oven and increasing the heat allows the puffs to reach their maximum height. They rise along with the temperature in the oven.*

# Apple Strudel

*Serves Eight*

*This is one of the desserts I delivered to the Rosie O'Donnell Show after her producers expressed interest in my dessert book, and I knew this strudel would not disappoint. The show soon ended, and the producers moved on—but they took my book with them—using it as their very first book club selection for their new show on The Food Network. I guess the strudel worked.*

## INGREDIENTS:

**4 cups finely sliced, peeled apples (about 1½–1¾ pounds fresh)**

**⅓ cup Splenda Granulated sweetener**

**¼ cup raisins, finely chopped**

**¼ cup pecans, finely chopped**

**1½ teaspoons cinnamon**

**1 tablespoon plain bread crumbs**

**6 sheets phyllo dough (12 × 16 inches)**

**Nonstick cooking spray**

**½ tablespoon butter, melted**

**1 tablespoon powdered sugar**

*Phyllo dough is a great low-fat replacement for pastry. Phyllo (or filo) dough can be found in the freezer section in grocery stores. Be sure to thaw the dough thoroughly before using and keep the sheets you're not working with covered with a damp cloth or plastic wrap to keep them from drying out.*

## PER SERVING

| | |
|---|---|
| Calories 160 | |
| Carbohydrate 26 grams | Total Fat 6 grams |
| Sugars 14 grams | Saturated Fat 1 gram |
| Fiber 3 grams | Protein 2 grams |
| | Sodium 75 milligrams |

Diabetic exchange = 1 Fruit, ½ Carbohydrate, 1 Fat
WW point comparison = 3 points

## STEPS:

1. Preheat oven to 350°F. Spray a baking sheet with nonstick cooking spray.

2. In a large bowl, combine apples and next 5 ingredients (sweetener through bread crumbs). Set aside.

3. Spread a large piece of plastic wrap or wax paper onto a large surface. Carefully lay 1 piece of the phyllo dough onto the work surface, with the long side closest to you. Lightly spray the entire sheet lightly with cooking spray. Lay another sheet of dough on top of the first. Spray again. Repeat until all 6 sheets are stacked. Spoon the apple mixture in a long strip across the center of the dough, leaving 3 inches on all sides. Starting with the long side of the dough that is closest to you, lift the empty dough up over the apples. Fold side ends and far side of dough up and over the apples to enclose. Carefully use the paper to help you turn the strudel, seam side down, onto the prepared baking sheet.

4. Brush with melted butter.

5. Bake 40–45 minutes or until the pastry is golden brown.

6. Cool slightly and sift powdered sugar over entire strudel. Best when served warm.

# Strawberry Shortcake

*Serves Eight*

*Strawberry shortcake is always a special treat. What makes this particular cake even better is that it only takes a short time to prepare. Using a reduced-fat baking mix makes it quick and easy to produce the tender sweet biscuits that will hold all those luscious fresh berries.*

INGREDIENTS:

**4 cups sliced strawberries**

**¼ cup Splenda Granulated sweetener**

**2 cups reduced-fat baking mix (like Bisquick Reduced-Fat)**

**⅓ cup Splenda Granulated sweetener**

**1 teaspoon baking powder**

**½ teaspoon baking soda**

**⅔ cup low-fat buttermilk**

**1½ tablespoons margarine or butter, melted**

**1 egg, beaten**

**1 teaspoon sugar (optional)**

**1½ cups light whipped topping, thawed**

*Who said strawberries owned shortcakes? Try substituting fresh peaches or other berries to give an old favorite a new twist.*

STEPS:

1. Preheat oven to 425°F. Spray a baking sheet with nonstick cooking spray.

2. In a medium bowl, toss strawberries with ¼ cup sweetener. Set aside.

3. In a large bowl, combine baking mix, ⅓ cup sweetener, baking powder, and baking soda.

4. Mix buttermilk and melted butter together and pour over dry ingredients. Stir with a spoon until dough comes together.

5. Remove dough from bowl and place on lightly floured surface. Knead dough 10 times; then pat or roll into even ½-inch thickness.

6. Using a 2½-inch round cutter or a glass, cut out shortcakes and transfer them to the prepared baking sheet. Gather scraps of dough together and cut out more cakes for a total of 8.

7. Brush with beaten egg and sprinkle a little sugar on each cake.

8. Bake for 12–15 minutes. Transfer to rack and let cool slightly.

9. To assemble shortcakes: Split each shortcake in half. Place the bottoms on dessert plates. Cover with ½ cup berries on each cake. Cover with top of each shortcake.

10. Top with 3 tablespoons light whipped topping and serve immediately.

**PER SERVING**

| | |
|---|---|
| Calories 195 | Total Fat 6 grams |
| Carbohydrate 31 grams | Saturated Fat 3 grams |
| Sugars 8 grams | Protein 3.5 grams |
| Fiber 2 grams | Sodium 420 milligrams |

Diabetic exchange = 1½ Carbohydrate, ½ Fruit
WW point comparison = 4 points

# Simple Sauces and Toppings

How do you make an ordinary dessert extraordinary? Just add a sauce or a topping. Sauces and toppings are a great way to create, dress up, or embellish your favorite treats. What I love about them, besides how professional they make everything look, is how easy they are to make and keep, and how little it takes to really jazz up any dessert. Unfortunately, with most sauces or toppers, that "little" embellishment really adds to the sugar, fat, and caloric content of the dessert. Not here, of course. These scrumptious sauces and toppings add a whole lot more pleasure to the dessert than to the numbers in the nutritional analysis. The berry sauces and brand new Super Simple Cherry Topping are fresh tasting and versatile and can be used on everything from plain cakes to ice cream and cheesecakes. Rich Custard Sauce takes fruit to a whole new level and my sweet Lemon Curd is a basic for fillings and frostings. You'll also find decadent Chocolate Fudge Sauce is terrific on just about everything (even on a spoon!). And last, but not least, the Orange Cream Cheese is the perfect complement to breads or muffins, and the Easy Chocolate Cream Frosting can dress up a chocolate cake or turn Chocolate Chocolate Chip Muffins into truly dangerous treats.

# Rich Custard Sauce

*Serves Nine*

*I love fresh fruit, especially berries. But fresh fruit for dessert, well—it's still just fresh fruit. But if you place some berries in a nice glass and pour on a little Rich Custard Sauce, voilà—real dessert. So simple, so good! You can use this sauce to doll up unfrosted cakes like the Citrus Chiffon Cake or your favorite angel food cake.*

INGREDIENTS:

**2 tablespoons Splenda Granulated sweetener**

**1 tablespoon cornstarch**

**2 egg yolks**

**1 cup 1% milk**

**¼ cup nonfat half-and-half**

**1½ teaspoons vanilla extract**

*For a delicious treat, add a touch of orange zest or 1 tablespoon of orange liqueur to this versatile sauce.*

STEPS:

1. Place sweetener, cornstarch, and egg yolks in a small saucepan. Whisk together until eggs have lightened in color and sweetener and cornstarch are dissolved. Whisk in milk and half-and-half.

2. Place pan on stove and turn heat to medium. Heat, stirring constantly, until mixture comes to a low boil. Turn heat down and let simmer 1 minute. Custard should be thick enough to coat a spoon but not as thick as pudding.

3. Whisk in vanilla and immediately remove from heat.

4. Pour into a bowl and cover with plastic wrap.

5. Cool and refrigerate until ready to serve.

**PER SERVING (2 TABLESPOONS)**

| | |
|---|---|
| Calories 35 | Total Fat 1.5 grams |
| Carbohydrate 3 grams | Saturated Fat 0.5 gram |
| Sugars 1 gram | Protein 2 grams |
| Fiber 0 grams | Sodium 15 milligrams |

Diabetic exchange = ¼ Low-Fat Milk
WW point comparison = 1 point

# Blueberry Sauce and Coulis

*Serves Eight*

*This would make a lovely gift. Once made and bottled, it will hold for up to two weeks in the refrigerator. This sauce is a wonderful complement to lemon desserts as well as good old vanilla ice cream.*

INGREDIENTS:

**2 cups fresh or frozen blueberries (1 pint)**

**¼ cup Splenda Granulated sweetener**

**⅓ cup cold water**

**2 teaspoons cornstarch**

**1 teaspoon lemon juice**

**1 tablespoon crème de cassis liqueur (optional)**

STEPS:

1. Place the berries in a heavy non-aluminum saucepan. Add remaining ingredients (except liqueur) and stir until cornstarch dissolves.

2. Place over medium heat and bring to a boil. Turn down heat and simmer for 1 minute, stirring constantly.

3. Remove from heat and stir in liqueur if desired.

BLUEBERRY COULIS VARIATION: Strain the blueberry sauce through a fine strainer or sieve, pressing on the fruit to drain all the liquid. Throw away pulp. Serving size for coulis is 2 tablespoons.

*Coulis, pronounced kool-ee, is a smooth or puréed sauce of fruit or vegetables. Fruit coulis are very popular with pastry chefs because they can be made with almost any fruit and are a mainstay for plated dessert presentations.*

---

**PER SERVING (3 TABLESPOONS)**

| | |
|---|---|
| Calories 20 | Total Fat 0 grams |
| Carbohydrate 5 grams | Saturated Fat 0 grams |
| Sugars 3 grams | Protein 0 gram |
| Fiber 1 gram | Sodium 0 milligrams |

Diabetic exchange = 1 Free Food
WW point comparison = 0 points

# Strawberry Sauce and Coulis

*Serves Eight*

*This is one of the most versatile sauces I've ever come across. Unstrained, it makes a nice chunky sauce for ice cream or plain cakes. Strained, it's a smooth fruit sauce (coulis) that's an elegant accompaniment to desserts such as Heavenly Cheesecake and Cold Strawberry Soufflé.*

INGREDIENTS:

**2 cups strawberries, fresh or frozen**

**⅓ cup Splenda Granulated sweetener**

**1 tablespoon lemon juice**

**½ cup water**

**2 teaspoons cornstarch**

**1 tablespoon orange liqueur (optional)**

STEPS:

1. Place the berries in a heavy non-aluminum saucepan. Add remaining ingredients (except liqueur) and stir until cornstarch dissolves. Place over medium heat and bring to a boil. Turn down and simmer for 1 minute, stirring constantly.

2. Remove from heat and stir in liqueur if desired.

STRAWBERRY COULIS VARIATION: Strain the strawberry sauce through a fine strainer or sieve, pressing on the fruit to drain all the liquid. Throw away pulp.

*For a dramatic and elegant presentation, drizzle, pool, or paint Strawberry Coulis onto plates before adding dessert. A squeeze bottle normally used for ketchup is a handy tool for drizzling sauces.*

PER SERVING (2 TABLESPOONS)

| | |
|---|---|
| Calories 15 | Total Fat 0 grams |
| Carbohydrate 3 grams | Saturated Fat 0 grams |
| Sugars 1 gram | Protein 0 grams |
| Fiber 0 grams | Sodium 0 milligrams |

Diabetic exchange = 1 Free Food
WW point comparison = 0 points

# Quick Raspberry Sauce

*Serves Eight*

*It doesn't get any quicker than this. No fancy ingredients are required for this easy sauce, whipped up in the microwave in just seconds. Drizzle Quick Raspberry Sauce over cakes or on cake plates for dramatic presentations, or simply use it on your favorite ice cream.*

INGREDIENTS:

**6 tablespoons low-sugar raspberry jam**

**6 tablespoons water**

**¼ cup Splenda Granulated sweetener**

STEPS:

1. Place all the ingredients in a small microwaveable bowl.

2. Heat for 30–45 seconds on high.

3. Stir until smooth. Use warm or cold.

*This recipe can be made with any low-sugar jam. I like Smucker's. It's just fruit, with 50 percent less sugar and calories than ordinary jam. Watch out for reduced-sugar or "fruit-only" jams that use concentrated fruit juices to make up for the reduction in sugar. They can have as much or even more sugar than regular jams.*

**PER SERVING (1 ½ TABLESPOONS)**

| | |
|---|---|
| Calories 16 | Total Fat 0 grams |
| Carbohydrate 4 grams | Saturated Fat 0 grams |
| Sugars 3 grams | Protein 0 grams |
| Fiber 0 grams | Sodium 0 milligrams |

Diabetic exchange = 1 Free Food
WW point comparison = 0 points

# Super Simple Cherry Topping

*Serves Seven*

*This quick and easy topping can be made effortlessly in just minutes and served on everything from pancakes to cheesecake (and that most certainly includes the Unbelievable Chocolate Cake on page 102). I can't imagine making this without the almond extract, but if you don't have any, don't worry, vanilla also works well.*

INGREDIENTS:

1 14.5-ounce can tart cherries, packed in water

¼ cup water

½ cup Splenda Granulated sweetener

1½ tablespoons cornstarch

1 tablespoon granulated sugar

½ teaspoon almond extract

STEPS:

1. Pour juice from cherries into a small saucepan. Add water, sweetener, cornstarch, and sugar, and stir. Add cherries. Place saucepan over medium heat and bring to a low boil. Cook 1 minute or until liquid clears. Stir in almond extract.

*Cherries are now considered a superfruit! High in healthy antioxidants, they are a delicious and powerful ally in the fight against heart disease, diabetes, and cancer.*

**PER SERVING**

| | |
|---|---|
| Calories 40 | Total Fat 0 grams |
| Carbohydrate 10 grams | Saturated Fat 0 grams |
| Sugars 6 grams | Protein 0 grams |
| Fiber 1 gram | Sodium 0 milligrams |

Diabetic exchange = ½ Fruit

WW point comparison = 1 point

# Chocolate Fudge Sauce

*Serves Eleven*

*This recipe made my day. I had tried other low-sugar fudge sauce recipes and was never quite satisfied because they were all missing the characteristic texture that sugar imparts. Then I saw a recipe that used maple syrup in place of sugar, and that idea piqued my interest. After trying the recipe (using Low-Calorie Log Cabin Syrup made with Splenda) and making a few modifications, I finally hit on a winner. Just like the best fudge sauces, this tightens up in the refrigerator. Heat gently in the microwave or on the stove before using.*

INGREDIENTS:

**2 ounces semisweet chocolate**

**2 tablespoons Dutch-process cocoa powder (like Hershey's Special Dark)**

**2 tablespoons sugar-free (or light) maple-flavored syrup**

**¼ cup Splenda Granulated sweetener**

**⅓ cup water**

**½ teaspoon vanilla extract**

STEPS:

1. Chop semisweet chocolate into small pieces.

2. Place in a medium-size microwaveable bowl. (You may also make this in a saucepan on the stove.)

3. Add remaining ingredients.

4. Heat in microwave on high for 45 seconds; chocolate will not be completely melted.

5. Remove and stir thoroughly until smooth. Add vanilla.

*Compare this Chocolate Fudge Sauce to Hershey's Chocolate Fudge Topping, which has 70 calories per tablespoon and 10 grams of sugar.*

**PER SERVING (1 TABLESPOON)**

| | |
|---|---|
| Calories 30 | Total Fat 1.5 grams |
| Carbohydrate 4 grams | Saturated Fat 1 gram |
| Sugars 0 grams | Protein 0 grams |
| Fiber 0 grams | Sodium 0 milligrams |

Diabetic exchange = ½ Fat

WW point comparison = 1 point

# Lemon Curd

*Serves Fourteen*

*This is a filling or topping that can easily be converted to a sauce. It is often used in place of jam on biscuits and as a filling for cakes or tarts. I use it to make a luscious lemon cream frosting for the Lemon Coconut Layer Cake on page 111. If you want to make a thick lemon sauce, simply thin the curd with some hot water and stir until smooth.*

## INGREDIENTS:

⅔ **cup lemon juice**

2 **tablespoons water**

1 **large egg, beaten**

1 **large egg yolk**

2 **tablespoons cornstarch**

⅔ **cup Splenda Granulated sweetener**

1 **tablespoon granulated sugar**

2 **tablespoons light butter**

## STEPS:

1. In a medium non-aluminum saucepan, thoroughly whisk together the first 7 ingredients (lemon juice through sugar).

2. Place pan on stove and turn heat to medium. Cook, whisking constantly, until mixture comes to a boil. Boil, whisking, for 1 minute. Mixture should be thick and clear.

3. Remove from the heat and stir in the butter. Cool.

*Mix a couple of tablespoons of lemon curd into softened light cream cheese for a delicious spread you can use on muffins and biscuits.*

## PER SERVING (1 TABLESPOON)

| | |
|---|---|
| Calories 25 | Total Fat 1.5 grams |
| Carbohydrate 4 grams | Saturated Fat 0.5 gram |
| Sugars 0 grams | Protein 0 grams |
| Fiber 0 grams | Sodium 0 milligrams |

Diabetic exchange = ¼ Carbohydrate

WW point comparison = 1 point

# Orange Cream Cheese

*Serves Eight*

*I served Orange Cream Cheese with my Pumpkin Pecan Bread (page 58), and all my tasters declared it a huge hit. This topping also complements fruit and bran muffins, biscuits, and mini-bagels.*

INGREDIENTS:

**4-ounce tub-style light cream cheese**

**1 tablespoon orange juice**

**2 teaspoons Splenda Granulated sweetener**

**1 teaspoon grated orange zest**

STEPS:

1. Place all the ingredients in a small bowl.

2. Beat until creamy. Orange Cream Cheese keeps well in the refrigerator for 1–2 weeks.

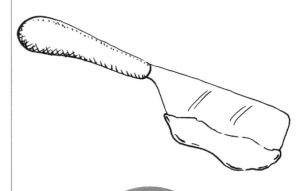

*So much tastier than butter, this Orange Cream Cheese has only 1/3 the calories and a fraction of the saturated fat.*

**PER SERVING (1 TABLESPOON)**

| | |
|---|---|
| Calories 30 | Total Fat 2.5 grams |
| Carbohydrate 1.5 grams | Saturated Fat 1 gram |
| Sugars 1 gram | Protein 1 gram |
| Fiber 0 grams | Sodium 65 milligrams |

Diabetic exchange = ½ Fat

WW point comparison = 1 point

# Whipped Cream Cheese Topping and Frosting

*Serves Eighteen*

*I first made this light whipped frosting to adorn my California Carrot Cake (page 105), only to find that the frosting was a star all by itself. Never a fan of heavy, cloying cream cheese frostings, I added a bit of light whipped topping to create a cream cheese frosting that's light, smooth, and fluffy but still retains that great cream cheese taste. After you try it, you'll surely find other uses for it (one of my readers told me she enjoyed it best straight out of the bowl).*

INGREDIENTS:

**8 ounces tub-style light cream cheese**

**4 ounces nonfat cream cheese**

**¼ cup Splenda Granulated sweetener**

**1 cup light whipped topping**

STEPS:

1. In a small mixing bowl, beat the cream cheeses with an electric mixer until smooth.

2. Add the sweetener and beat for 1 minute longer.

3. On slow speed, beat in the whipped topping, beating briefly, just until smooth.

PER SERVING (2 TABLESPOONS)

| | |
|---|---|
| Calories 40 | Total Fat 2 grams |
| Carbohydrate 3 grams | Saturated Fat 1.5 grams |
| Sugars 2 grams | Protein 2 grams |
| Fiber 0 grams | Sodium 80 milligrams |

Diabetic exchange = 1 Fat

WW point comparison = 1 point

# Easy Chocolate Cream Frosting

*Serves Nine*

*This is a quick way to turn light whipped topping into a nice chocolate topping or frosting. The recipe makes enough to frost a 9-inch round or square cake or a dozen cupcakes.*

INGREDIENTS:

**1¾ cups light whipped topping, thawed**

**2 tablespoons Dutch-process cocoa powder (like Hershey's Special Dark)**

**¼ cup Splenda Granulated sweetener**

STEPS:

1. Place whipped topping in a medium bowl.

2. Gently fold in the cocoa powder and sweetener. Overmixing will break down cream topping.

3. Refrigerate until use. Spread or spoon onto cakes or muffins.

*Because frostings either rely on lots of fat (like butter or melted chocolate) or powdered sugar for bulk, cutting the fat and the sugar is tricky. I have found light whipped topping makes a perfect base.*

**PER SERVING**

Calories 35

Carbohydrate 4 grams

  Sugars 1 gram

  Fiber 0 grams

Total Fat 1.5 grams

  Saturated Fat 1.5 grams

Protein 0 grams

Sodium 0 milligrams

Diabetic exchange = ½ Carbohydrate

WW point comparison = 1 point

# Index

# About the Author

Marlene Koch is a registered dietitian, professional cooking instructor, and nutrition educator who has specialized in delicious food and healthy lifestyles for over 20 years. Thus, when Marlene realized she couldn't bake a delicious cake without sugar for her stepdaughter newly diagnosed with type 2 diabetes, she set out to find the sweet solution! Marlene is now the foremost authority on cooking with sugar substitutes and the author of three best-selling healthy, low-sugar cookbooks.

Marlene, a popular guest on QVC, *loves* to teach, and to eat! As a nutrition educator Marlene has spoken on behalf of the American Diabetes and American Heart Associations, and her television and radio appearances have included affiliates for ABC, NBC, CBS, FOX, and Shaw TV (Vancouver) as well as radio stations nationwide. Her books and incredible recipes have also received star billing everywhere from the *Today Show* to the Food Network as well as in print publications such as *Cooking Light, Diabetic Cooking Magazine, Her Sports, Men's Fitness*, and across the web from iVillage to Children with Diabetes and dLife.com.

Marlene resides near San Francisco with her two sweet-loving sons and husband and remains an active member of the American Dietetic Association, the Food & Culinary Professionals association, and the International Association of Culinary Professionals. On the web she can be found at www.marlenekoch.com and as the Food and Nutrition Expert for Destination Diabetes at www.destinationdiabetes.com.

If you have enjoyed *Marlene Koch's Unbelievable Desserts with Splenda Sweetener*, you will also enjoy:

*Fantastic Food with Splenda: 160 Great Recipes for Meals Low in Sugar, Fat, and Calories*
This fantastic book of 160 recipes showcases the versatility of Splenda sweetener by taking it *way* beyond dessert! Sweet Cinnamon French Toast, Classic Three Bean Salad, Sweet and Sour Chicken, Tomato Ginger Jam, Boston Baked Beans, and loads of dessert recipes, including Creamy Lemon Bars and Dark Chocolate Mousse, make this a book you will reach for over and over again. With information on how to lower the fat and slash the sugar in your favorite foods, healthy has never tasted better! Terrific for all diets, including calorie and fat controlled, carb conscious, and diet programs such as South Beach and Weight Watchers. Complete nutritional analysis with diabetic exchanges and comparisons to Weight Watchers' points.

ISBN 1-59077-021-8 M. Evans and Company 2004 Hardcover 285 pages

*Marlene Koch's Sensational Splenda Recipes: Over 375 Recipes Low in Sugar, Fat, and Calories*
This truly is the ultimate low-sugar cookbook! Includes over 125 brand new recipes in addition to all the recipes from the first edition of *Unbelievable Desserts* and *Fantastic Food with Splenda*, ensuring you will find recipes to love for every meal and every occasion, including cocktails! Also features invaluable tips for every type of Splenda—including Splenda-Sugar blends—for delicious foods and beverages such as your own Homemade Hot Chocolate Mix and sugar-free Coffee Liqueur to Oatmeal Cookie Pancakes, Asian Peanut Slaw, and Spicy Orange Beef, and even more incredible desserts like classic Lemon Meringue Pie, Dark Chocolate Brownies, and Strawberry Topped New York Cheesecake. Complete nutritional analysis with diabetic exchanges and Weight Watchers' point comparisons.

IBSN 1-59077-138-9 M. Evans 2006 Hardcover 504 pages